Identity in the Age of Cloud Computing:

The next-generation Internet's impact on business, governance and social interaction

J.D. Lasica
Rapporteur

THE ASPEN) INSTITUTE

Communications and Society Program
Charles M. Firestone
Executive Director
Washington, DC
2009

Charles M. Firestone

Executive Director

Patricia K. Kelly

Assistant Director

The Aspen Institute
One Dupont Circle, NW
Suite 700
Washington, DC 20036

Published in the United States of America in 2009
by The Aspen Institute

Contents

APPENDIX

Foreword

Cloud computing has quickly become a buzzword in the information and communications technology (ICT) world. It refers to the myriad of information and communications activities that are increasingly taking place in the network, broadly defined. Like the migration of electricity in the early 1900s from local generation to an electrical grid with metered service, the cloud signals the movement of hard and soft functions such as storage, software applications and services to an off premises service industry.

The clearest example would be a company that had its product endorsed by Oprah Winfrey one day and had to increase its server capacity the next day to prevent its website from crashing. Renting the huge server capacity of a major provider for the time needed, the firm would save revenues, reputation, and unneeded capital expenditures.

Coming after decades of increased capacity and expectations from the desktop at the network's edge, the burgeoning acceptance of the cloud as a way of doing business raises a number of interesting and important questions for the broader public. What control do we have over our identities, security, and privacy? How will it change economic and business models? What are the implications for governance and cyber-security?

In the summer of 2008, the Aspen Institute Communications and Society Program convened 28 leaders and experts from the ICT, financial, government, academic, and public policy sectors to better understand the implications of cloud computing, and where appropriate, to suggest policies for the betterment of society.

This report by J.D. Lasica provides some background on the topic as it gives the reader the benefit of the considerable insights that emerged from the roundtable dialogue. It begins, as the conference did, with a description and definition of the cloud. Computing has evolved over time and has become increasingly more portable and personal—giving the average individual computing capabilities by way of laptops, smartphones, or any other peripheral device that connects to the internet.

As data (previously stored on PCs) begins to migrate into the cloud, every aspect of life and business as we know it will be impacted. But exactly how is subject to informed conjecture. As Bill Coleman states in the following report, "We're about where we were with the automobile, electrical power and radio in the 1910's and 1920's, where all we knew was what they were, but we were just beginning to understand what that meant to improve our quality of life in the future."

Throughout the sessions personal identity arose as a significant issue. Get it right and many services are enabled and enhanced. The group tended to agree that a user-centric open identity network system is the right approach at this point. It could give everyone the opportunity to manage their own identity, customize it for particular purposes, (i.e., give only so much information to an outsider as is necessary for them to transact with you in the way you need), and make it scalable across the Net. Other ways of looking at it include scaling the social web by allowing the individual to have identity as a kind of service rather than, as Lasica writes, "something done to you by outside interests."

From identity, which has tentacles in each of the ensuing issues, the report describes and analyzes the implication of the cloud on money, commerce, and personal well-being. There are 12 features of the cloud economy alone. Businesses, for example, will no longer incur massive start-up costs to lay technical infrastructure and operate servers. Instead, they will move to a variable cost model, using server resources and paying for them only as needed. This reduces the barriers of entry, allowing for expansion to new markets, experimentation and innovation.

As it explored the implications for governance and national security, the group spent significant time on defining and protecting the line between individual liberties and the power of the state, an issue complicated by the many jurisdictions that information may touch on its path from source to recipient. As governments will no doubt have to get involved in setting standards and, indeed, laws in this field, there must also be vigilance to assure the right balance of liberty and power.

In this as in the other topics of the report, Lasica goes beyond the roundtable discussion by providing context and outside research to acknowledge the complexity of the issues, yet organizes the topics in understandable conceptual language with examples. These are increasingly important issues placed in a more complicated setting, and I am pleased that we are able to present them in a clear and forthright manner.

Acknowledgments

I want to thank McKinsey & Company for its leadership and senior level support in developing this Roundtable, and our corporate sponsors Cassatt Corporation, Google, Text 100 and Intel. James Manyika, Bill Coleman, John Seely Brown, Shona Brown, Aedhmar Hynes and Gilman Louie provided suggestions and assistance in designing the program. A special thank you goes to J.D. Lasica, our talented rapporteur, for compiling such a complex set of discussions into a coherent, informative and well-written report. Finally, I thank Kiahna Williams, project manager, and Tricia Kelly, assistant director of the Communications and Society Program, for their efforts in producing this report and the Roundtable itself.

Charles M. Firestone
Executive Director
Communications and Society Program
Washington, D.C.
March 2009

IDENTITY IN THE AGE OF CLOUD COMPUTING:

THE NEXT-GENERATION INTERNET'S IMPACT ON BUSINESS, GOVERNANCE AND SOCIAL INTERACTION

J.D. Lasica

Identity in the Age of Cloud Computing:

The next-generation Internet's impact on business, governance and social interaction

J.D. Lasica

Introduction

I am whatever I say I am.

— *Video Republic,* a European
Cultural Foundation video[1]

Identity—the very essence of who we are and how we interact with others—is in the middle of a period of extraordinary tumult. The Internet and a host of new communications technologies have transformed the concept of identity and redefined our relationships to businesses, governments and constantly churning networks of friends and peers.

Growing numbers of digital natives now define themselves by their Web presence as well as their real-world presence. Indeed, they move seamlessly from their online to offline lives, and they expect to assert who they are on their own terms.

Call it the audacity of self-identity. I am whatever I say I am.

Now couple that notion of empowerment, enabled by a growing suite of Web 2.0 tools, with the cloud—our shorthand for a vast, always-on, accessible, broadband-enabled next-generation Internet that is fast approaching. The cloud holds out transformative possibilities for culture, commerce, national security, public life and personal interactions on a scale we are only beginning to fathom.

In the summer of 2008, twenty-eight people from private industry, government, venture funds and academia gathered in Aspen, Colorado to begin charting a roadmap for identity in the cloud. Their specific policy proposals appear at the end of this report.

Participants found common ground in identifying deep, long-term trends that are leading inexorably to an era of cheap, easily accessible computing and communications where individuals throughout the world will access information and empowering new tools as easily as they place a phone call today. That vision extends far beyond Web 2.0 social networking, a precursor of the cloud, to a future in which a connected global network of identifiable people and things transforms most of the elements of societal, commercial and government interaction as we know them today. Participants approached each of these transformations through the lens of identity in the new cultural landscape.

As mass markets give way to millions of niche markets and as the culture changes from one in which companies push products to passive consumers into one in which empowered users pull down products and services that meet their needs, society will collectively take part in determining another transformative shift: the extent to which people are able to define themselves—to assert their own interests and preferences—or have their identity shaped by outside forces. Today, these battles are playing out on a smaller scale in Washington and in foreign capitals where debates are being joined over online behavioral targeting, access to ISP [Internet service provider] records and net neutrality.

Identity, privacy and security all interconnect and will intersect in even deeper ways in the years ahead.

It appears that the full cloud, in its startling richness, remains at least a decade away, and the changes outlined in this report will not happen suddenly. But the roundtable participants believe they will happen. Indeed, many of the cloud's shapes and forms are now becoming visible, and participants spent three days identifying and anticipating the key issues that will need to be addressed as the cloud materializes. Over time, the cloud will transform our approach to such fundamental concepts as search, commerce, money and security on a global basis.

The roundtable undertook the task of defining the forces driving the cloud forward and mapping those drivers to the real-world implications for commerce, governance and personal well-being. The sooner these issues are addressed in practical terms, the more likely marketplace forces can be shaped—by businesses, civic groups, individuals, NGOs, think tanks and governments—to advance the public good. Conversely, failure to consider these matters at an early stage could have momentous consequences.

In the end, the roundtable participants welcomed the advent of these large-scale disruptive changes to our lives, given the possibilities for social betterment that the cloud holds for wide swaths of humanity. We are poised on the frontier of something remarkable.

Why the Cloud Matters

> "At the end of August [2008], as Hurricane Gustav threatened the coast of Texas, the Obama campaign called the Red Cross to say it would be routing donations to it via the Red Cross home page. Get your servers ready—our guys can be pretty nuts, Team Obama said. Sure, sure, whatever, the Red Cross responded. We've been through 9/11, Katrina, we can handle it. The surge of Obama dollars crashed the Red Cross website in less than 15 minutes."[2] —*Newsweek*

The New York-based tech start-up Animoto, which lets users create professional-quality, MTV-style videos using their own images and licensed music, was averaging 5,000 users a day until it suddenly received a burst of new users who discovered it through Facebook. Its traffic surged to 750,000 visitors over three days. The number of servers Animoto was running on jumped from 50 to 3,500 during that span of time. "It was just numbers we never imagined we would ever see," chief technology officer Stevie Clifton told a Seattle newspaper. "It was fun and scary and pretty cool." Thanks to Amazon Web Services, Animoto's servers did not crash, because Animoto does not have any servers. It outsources its computing power to Amazon.com and pays only for what it uses. The ten-employee company is now expanding. Amazon CEO Jeff Bezos touts Animoto as the poster company for cloud computing.[3]

The tales of the Red Cross and Animoto neatly sum up the contrast between the former economy and the emerging cloud economy.

If the Internet economy is an apt descriptor of the changes taking place around us today, then the term cloud economy could justly be ascribed to the still larger global disruptions ahead. Google CEO Eric Schmidt has called this "the cloud computing age."

What is the cloud, where did it come from, and what does it portend?

Information technology's steady evolution

The computing industry has evolved rapidly over the years. Mainframe computers, which began it all, were centralized with a professional class accessing information from terminals with little computing power; data transfer often took place on foot, as people carried floppy disks from one machine to another. Mainframes gave way to minicomputers (chiefly used in labs and factories in the 1970s), which begat personal computers, which brought processing power to the individual's desktop with basic applications like Word documents and spreadsheets. The personal computing revolution became portable with laptops, handheld devices and smartphones.

With every evolutionary step, computing's underlying architecture became more distributed. As the Internet became widely adopted in the 1990s, personal computers not only stored data locally but downloaded and exchanged data all over the Web.

We are now in the middle of another shift. As the Pew Internet & American Life Project put it in a September 2008 study:

> Recent evolutions in information technology have led to a more distributed computing environment, while also reviving the utility of centralized storage. The growth in high-speed data lines, the falling cost of storage, the advent of wireless high-speed networks, the proliferation of handheld devices that can access the Web—together, these factors mean that users now can store data on a server that likely resides in a remote data center. Users can then access the data from their own computer, someone else's desktop computer, a laptop that wirelessly connects to the internet, or a handheld device.[4]

This is where cloud computing enters the picture, as users at home and in the workplace have begun to manage their data, run applications, crunch numbers and operate entire enterprises on a virtual platform in the sky. While the actual computing may be taking place on the next block or on the other side of the world, to the user it looks as if it is happening on the screen in front of you.

The leap to the cloud echoes what occurred more than a century ago, author Nicholas Carr said in his keynote talk at the 2008 Xconomy conference. In the nineteenth century, companies often generated their own power with steam engines and dynamos. But with the rise of reliable electric utilities, companies stopped generating their own power and plugged into a shared electrical grid. Information technology is undergoing a similar evolution today.[5]

The public may not be familiar with the term, but many are already doing cloud computing. We have been using Web applications for years without any concern about where the applications actually run. The Pew study found that 69 percent of Americans connected to the Web—and especially younger users—already use some kind of cloud service, such as Web email (Gmail, Yahoo! Mail or Hotmail), online data storage (IDrive, Mozy, Box.net) or online software. For example, Google Docs offers Web-based office tools such as word processing and spreadsheets. Zoho, a start-up in Pleasanton, California, offers an even more robust suite of office productivity tools. Del.icio.us offers an easy way to access bookmarks online. Bloglines and Google Reader are Web-based RSS readers. Tens of millions of us have uploaded videos to YouTube and sent photos to Flickr, SmugMug, Photobucket and other hosting sites.

The cloud has become our entertainment network: we are spending hundreds of millions of hours on sites like YouTube, Hulu and Flickr. The cloud has become our social network: Facebook, MySpace, Bebo, hi5 and similar sites now claim hundreds of millions of members. The cloud has become our virtual library: when we do a Google search we are fingering the cloud. The cloud has become our workbench: we manage projects in Basecamp, share large files with Pando, tweak photos in online photo editors like Adobe Photoshop Express and Picnik, and edit videos online with JayCut and Jumpcut. The cloud has become our development network: open source programmers trade code on sites like *SourceForge.net* and *Drupal.org*.

The term cloud computing, which came into wide use in tech circles only in early 2007, does have a specific, technical meaning. It refers to a collection of resources—applications, platforms, raw computing power and storage, and managed services (like antivirus detection)—delivered over the Internet. One Forrester Research analyst defined it as "a pool of abstracted, highly scalable, and managed compute infrastructure capable of hosting end-customer applications and billed by consumption."[6] Gartner Group defined cloud computing as "a style of computing where massively scalable, IT-enabled capabilities are provided 'as a ser-vice' to external customers using Internet technologies."[7]

Thus, in this strict sense, the cloud refers to virtual servers, distrib-uted hosting and shared resources available over the Internet. Today cloud computing is in its infancy, with a slew of vendors both large and small offering full-blown hosting infrastructure (hardware as a service), others offering online applications and still others offering business solutions (software as a service or SaaS).

The pioneer in the field, Amazon Web Services [AWS], offers two main flavors of cloud computing, renting storage space and access to companies like on-the-fly time share units. You can set up an online storefront by using EC2 (for Elastic Compute Cloud) to run whatever applications you want on its Linux machines, or use its S3 (for Simple Storage Service) to park your data. The service is cheap: a virtual machine starts at 10 cents per hour. As *Wired* magazine put it:

> Instead of building cute apps and ladling them out to the masses—the Google and Microsoft model—Amazon is delivering silicon power to the people. [Amazon CEO Jeff] Bezos is fueling a flotilla of nimble, aggressive entrepreneurs, including frontier types chaf-ing inside gilded prisons like the Googleplex. For them, AWS is a launch pad, not just for the next million Facebook apps, but also for personal live TV channels, virtual desktops, pay-by-the-mile auto insurance, and no doubt plenty of things no one has thought of yet.[8]

While Amazon's utility computing solution chiefly targets small businesses and consumers, companies such as Salesforce.com and Netsuite are targeting businesses of all sizes with both virtual hosting and software suites to run their data. VMware, Dell, AT&T, Microsoft and IBM are among the vendors offering cloudplexes or selling tools to create clouds. Other companies are now scrambling to offer a cloud platform or cloud services.

But many people now accept a broader meaning for the cloud, and this is the context in which the roundtable tackled the subject.

More than a decade ago Oracle CEO Larry Ellison declared that the network would become the computer, and many people now refer to the emerging next-generation Internet as "the cloud." One should think of the cloud not just literally, as an information technology infrastructure, but as a metaphor for this new frontier of democratizing possibilities that these disruptive new communication technologies herald.

An SAP white paper released in September 2008 warned that policymakers are not aware of the dramatic economic impact of the "Future Internet," as the paper calls the cloud. The report concluded: "The next generation of the Internet enabled by software will lead to the most significant changes in the economy in the next decade. It will drive productivity gains in many industries and shape the future of the services sector in all knowledge-based economies."[9]

At the Stanford Summit in July 2008, Anna Ewing, executive vice president and chief information officer of Nasdaq, invited people to think of the cloud as putting high-powered enterprise technology in the hands of the masses via the Internet. Russ Daniels of Hewlett-Packard suggested the key ingredient is virtualization—using someone else's computer to do the heavy lifting for you.[10] Polly Sumner of Salesforce.com said the smallest retail store can now use software as a service to run its financials and manage customer relationships in the cloud, while entrepreneurs will build processes and a new generation of applications we cannot even guess at yet.

In other words, what the cloud is may be less interesting than what the cloud does—or could do.

The New York Times wanted to convert 11 million articles dating from the newspaper's founding in 1851 through 1989 to make them available through its website search engine. The *Times* scanned in the stories, converted them to TIFF files, then uploaded the files to Amazon's S3, taking up four terabytes of space. "The *Times* didn't coordinate the job with Amazon—someone in IT just signed up for the service on the Web using a credit card," IDG News Service reported. Then, using Amazon's EC2 computing platform, the *Times* ran a PDF conversion application that converted the 4TB of TIFF data into 1.5TB of PDF files. Using Amazon's computers, the job took about 24 hours.[11]

When Nasdaq wanted to launch a new service called Market Replay to sell historic data for stocks and funds, it turned to S3 to host the data and created a small reader application using Adobe's AIR technology that let users pull in the required data. The expense of storing all that data on

Nasdaq's own servers would have been prohibitive. Instead, by offloading the data to the cloud, Nasdaq now has a modest new revenue stream.[12]

Other examples abound. Medical robotics firm Intuitive Surgical and recruitment services provider Jobscience use Salesforce.com's cloud environment to create new applications.[13] Pharmaceutical companies tap into Amazon Web Services to calculate simulations; the U.S. Marine Corps is using it to reduce its IT sites from 175 to about 100, and *The Washington Post* used it to turn Hillary Clinton's White House schedule during her husband's presidency, more than 17,000 pages, into a searchable database within twenty-four hours. The European consultancy Sogeti has used a cloud built by IBM to test new ideas and cobble together an IT system for a company-wide brainstorming event.[14]

To handle this burgeoning demand for the cloud by businesses and consumers, bigger and more energy-efficient data centers—7,000 in the United States alone so far—are being built. Besides Amazon, Google reportedly has two million servers running around the world. Yahoo! is busy building huge server farms, and Microsoft is adding up to 35,000 servers a month in places like its data center outside of Chicago, which covers 500,000 square feet at a cost of $500 million, with plans to hold 400,000 servers.[15]

But as much as this sounds like cloud computing is becoming more centralized, "that's a trap we shouldn't fall into," Michael DeNoma of Standard Chartered Bank of Singapore told the roundtable. "You have these central resources for computing power, and ultimately it's a distributed resource. That means anyone can use it."

This, then, is the new computing ecosystem: data centers serving as huge factories for computing services on an industrial scale; software being delivered as a service over the Internet; wireless networks linking all of this together, letting us access data, services—and each other.

But this is only the beginning. As the cloud becomes an integral part of the global economy, the 2007 Aspen Institute roundtable report, "The Rise of Collective Intelligence: Decentralized Co-Creation of Value as a New Paradigm of Commerce and Culture," predicted:

> All forms of content will be digitized and flowing through IP-based networks where data, audio and video have converged. As this happens, most of the applications and data storage that now reside on PCs and local servers will migrate to The Cloud, and com-

puting will become a commodity utility service. Vendors will supply capacity on-demand. As this happens, Web 2.0 will extend into all aspects of commercial interaction as the pull model of commerce becomes the norm with Web 3.0.[16]

If and when this occurs, the cloud will significantly alter many institutions and businesses as we know them today (as voice, video and data eventually converge in the cloud). The 2008 roundtable participants surveyed this longer time horizon and considered the impact the cloud will have on issues of identity, national security, money, commerce and personal well-being.

Early stages of the march toward the cloud

William T. Coleman III, founder of Cassatt Corporation, laid out his vision for the roundtable this way: "The Internet has changed the nature of computing away from interacting with machines or programs and toward a model where you can interact with other human beings in a one-to-one, a many-to-many or an anyone-to-anything-to-everyone-relationship. Anybody can reach anybody in real time in a space-independent and even time-independent way at no cost as long as they can get on the Internet. This changes the entire nature of the human dialogue. It is, in fact, the third step in the acceleration of human communication and knowledge accumulation which was proceeded by the invention of speech and the printing press. This is the first power of the Internet, free reach, and it will ultimately change and improve almost every aspect of the human conversation."

> **"...the first power of the Internet, free reach, ...will ultimately change and improve almost every aspect of the human conversation."**
>
> *William T. Coleman III*

"We're at an inflection point in which we are about to commoditize all of computing as we have known it by turning it into the cloud," Coleman said. "Cloud computing will become the platform for the Web just as the telephone system has been the platform for voice communication. For the next generation, the cloud will power the emergence of the Web platform that will ultimately serve as a sort of a dashboard for life, letting us create our own Web presence, where our virtual and physical identities merge."

Coleman contended that after free reach there are two other properties of the Internet: straight-through processing and transparency. When combined with social networking and identity to extend reach and enable yet unseen capabilities to empower consumers, the Internet will change how companies do business and lead to significant productivity increases. "The cloud will enable us to create designer products one at a time based on what my customer wants through the whole cycle of commerce in real time. It will dramatically accelerate the move from a push to a pull model of business, and that is the economic engine that is going to drive all of this. We will see higher levels of productivity at dramatically lower costs. The more you improve productivity, the more income everyone has to buy other services and outsource tasks to developing economies and address the underserved of the world. That creates a virtuous cycle—the pie gets bigger. In short, the cloud will unleash powerful forces that will transform all aspects of life and society."

But it will take two to three decades to arrive at the full-blown cloud. Today we are just at the beginning. "We're about where we were with the automobile, electrical power and radio in the 1910s and 1920s, where all we knew was what they were, but we were just beginning to understand what that meant to improve our quality of life in the future," Coleman said. For the cloud to become all-pervasive, we must first figure out how to overcome barriers around trust, reliability, control and security.

Over the next decade, said Coleman, innovators will create applications and new business models that pave the way for commercial transactions to move from a push to a pull model. "For that to happen, we have to solve identity," he said. "I'm not going to actually put myself out there in an e-commerce world unless I feel I have some control over who gets to see what parts of my identity." Thus, customers will be given more freedom to specify the kinds of products and services they need and to assert a measure of control over their own identities.

For that to happen, Coleman said, "The goal is to be able to access anything at any moment and view it through any device that can get onto the network, while knowing that my identity is safe and under my control. I don't want to think about the operating system or interoperability or the tools or applications I'm using."

Who will ultimately own or control the cloud? Most likely, no one. But many companies will exploit it financially. Today a lot of suppliers and vendors are emerging, chiefly from the technology sector. But you can be sure that the telecommunications and cable industries will follow suit before too long. "They're all accessing data and performing computational processing on it," Coleman said. "In a world where everything digital is IP-based, there's no difference between voice, video or data, and soon between our mobile and online experiences. It is all content, generated, manipulated and stored on computers and transmitted over the networks in a generic fashion. So all the service providers (telcos, cable, ASP, ISP, SaaS and portals) will be in the same business 10 years from now, and that's going to result in a huge battle for dominance leading to a massive consolidation."

One key feature of cloud computing is the pay-per-use model, that is, metered billing by quantity or quality of services consumed. While one version of cloud computing, enterprise software as a service, relies on a traditional subscription model with upfront fees and a long-term contract, utility computing—offered by Amazon Web Services and aimed at the masses—relies on a pay-per-use model. A small business like Animoto, which scaled very quickly from 50 to 3,500 servers, pays for use of those additional servers only when they are needed.

Factors driving the cloud forward

Coleman identified three major factors driving adoption of cloud computing:

- *Cost savings.* The economics of running large data centers is "unsustainable" for corporations, with server resources often idle eighty-five percent of the time. One of Coleman's clients, he said, estimates it will save $1 billion a year by moving to a cloud solution. Small companies will achieve substantial savings by offloading IT costs to the cloud.

- *Complexity of IT operations.* IT complexity has increased dramatically as applications become more integrated, changes require significant planning, profiling and testing and making even the smallest changes involves coordinating process changes across several organizations. This complexity escalates cost and reduces agility in a compounding way.

- *Competitive pressure to innovate.* "The innovation of new business models and new ways of gaining value is going to accelerate and be facilitated in the cloud, increasing the pressures to change and evolve just to survive, let alone to maintain the pace of growth," Coleman said.

James Manyika, senior partner at McKinsey & Company, pointed to another factor: the impact of the cloud on energy and power. Information technology's carbon footprint amounts to about two percent of global carbon emissions and is on course to rise to three percent—larger than the impact of the airline industries. When companies adopt virtualization technologies and thus lower on-site energy consumption, IT's footprint should go down dramatically. "The cloud is part of the solution," he said.

Arjun Gupta, founder of TeleSoft Partners, echoed that and called for a national program to build out a new networked smart grid to deliver electricity from suppliers to consumers using digital technology to save energy and costs. Such a modernized electricity network is being promoted by many as a way to address energy independence and combat global warming. "To reach Web 3.0, we will need a grid that goes from a one-way broadcast model to a true two-way model," he said. Life in the cloud will be rife with hundreds of millions of Internet-enabled sensors—in appliances, houses, cars, clothing, medical devices and roadways—letting us access, analyze and manage information in real time. Smart power grids and better traffic management are among the near-term benefits. Said Gupta: "Once you get this infrastructure out to every end point, a lot of passive elements that we have today can become active elements on a daily basis, and so you're rebalancing the whole system."

Esther Dyson, chairman of EDventure Holdings, said new business models will have a huge impact on how quickly the cloud is adopted: "Do you charge by the time? Do you charge by periods of access? Do you charge per transaction? What is being paid for and what is being offered for free? Will people donate free labor to filter and curate all this community stuff? What are the incentives and disincentives? How will intellectual property come into play when two sets of data or applications are involved? There are still a lot of questions and many different answers, some of which will work."

Michael DeNoma pointed to sociological factors that will drive the cloud forward: "The divergence between what our employees can do at home and what they can do with applications in the workplace continues to broaden, and they don't get it. They think, 'How can I do Facebook and Google at home and then I come to work and I need a week of training just to handle a customer's account?' So in financial services I think you'll see a move toward the cloud providing very substantial benefits."

Padmasree Warrior, chief technology officer of Cisco Systems, cited two other factors that will drive adoption of the cloud. First, large companies need to deploy new applications quickly and flexibly, and that is becoming more difficult across scattered branch offices running their operations on different sets of servers. Second, there are green factors, including lower power consumption, a smaller carbon footprint and space issues. Energy in the enterprise is made up of separate components today—lights, elevators, servers—but they will be equipped with networked sensors and react more intelligently in new designs.

"We may have reached the point where it no longer makes sense to think about hardware and software," she said. "Both need to be blended to offer new services."

Public vs. private clouds

Warrior foresees three stages of cloud formation.

In the first stage, which society is just entering, many large companies will offload their IT operations to their own "private clouds," with data and enterprise applications running on secure offsite data centers and linked to the company's offices through an encrypted pipeline over the public Internet.

Next, enterprise-class clouds will emerge, as companies will need to move data or applications from their private cloud to an external cloud. "You need standards to make that happen," she said, for instance, protocols for sharing data among pharmaceutical companies. Some are already calling for a "cloud computing consortium" to hash out the basic rules.

After that, Warrior predicts the rise of the "Inter-Cloud," a public or semi-public global town square in the sky where people and companies would share data, media, mash-ups and applications with the proper permission levels. Just as the Internet is a network of networks with a common set of rules, the Inter-Cloud would require clouds to play nice with each other, and that would necessitate a much more sophisticated and robust set of standards for interoperability—an inter-industry cross-platform operating system—than anything now on the cloud planners' white boards.

While clouds and cloud customers may naturally want to mingle so that data can be shared and mashed up, cloud operators may have other ideas. "I think the conditions around cloud platforms are such that the reflex is to define strong boundaries and assure security, not to enable robust interoperability," said John Seely Brown, director emeritus of Xerox PARC and independent co-chair of the Deloitte Center for Edge Innovation. "The idea of having multiple identities and being able to take your information with you and plug in anywhere is going to be resisted in some quarters."

Daniel Burton, senior vice president of global public policy for Salesforce.com, said there will be both public and private clouds, "but the public cloud is where the action is because it's accessible through the Internet and it has the potential for extraordinary innovation because of all the testing, trying things out, building on it." When things shake out, he said, a multitude of companies will be running their operations on a handful of cloud platforms. While many companies will continue to rely on their own data centers, he suggested that the race would go to the swift and nimble who innovate, rely on outside resources (third-party clouds) and pay only for what they need.

Aedhmar Hynes, CEO of Text100 Public Relations, made the important point that many of the assumptions about the build-out of the cloud comes from a Western perspective, while other regions of the world, particularly China, hold a very different view of how to deal with businesses and citizens in the next-generation Internet, and that needs to be respected.

Identity Meets the Cloud

Now that the Internet has brought us within easy reach of each other, the role of identity has taken on heightened prominence in social interactions, commercial transactions and governance. The ways we interact online—and, in surprising ways, offline—have changed significantly in recent years and stand to evolve in new directions in the near future.[17]

The roundtable examined several issues that new trends in technology and communications are bringing to the fore:

- how identity intersects with issues of privacy, security, anonymity, authentication, accountability and reputation;

- how identity maps to different contexts such as commerce, the local community, online communities, transactions, governmental interactions and virtual worlds;

- how concepts such as persistent identity, multiple identities, identity theft and reputation systems play out;

- the broad implications of a user-centric global identity system that empowers people to manage their own identities.

When the Web first became a mass phenomenon around 1993, we were all free to take on whatever persona appealed to us. To this day, many people use an online alias or pseudonym for their online forays while visiting websites, posting comments to forums or bulletin boards, or chatting with strangers. (While much of the mischief on the Net has been ascribed to anonymity, it is also important to point out that anonymity functions as a cloak to protect bloggers and others expressing dissenting political views within repressive regimes.) For some, that dichotomy between online persona and real-world identity proved empowering and exhilarating. But others quickly abused the freedoms that accompanied anonymity and pseudonymity. The early architects of the Web, who did not build in an "identity" component, could hardly be faulted for not foreseeing the onslaught of bad actors: scam artists, identity thieves, child predators, money launderers, spammers and other unsavory characters. Today, it is estimated that as much as eighty percent of email traffic is spam.

At the outset of the Web, "no one gave a lot of thought to putting identityware into the network," John Clippinger, a senior fellow at the Berkman Center, said. For the most part, the Web was an open, gift-exchange system between known or benign parties. "Clearly, that has changed," Clippinger added, with the onset of malicious actors releasing malware, viruses, phishing and pharming sites and with spammers taking on hundreds of identities. Today, whom we trust is no longer a simple proposition.

Between 2002 and 2005, something fundamental changed with online identity: the onset of the social Web. Blogging became a mainstream activity, and with it came a different mindset. With few exceptions, bloggers found the need to stand behind their words. They needed to tie their online musings to their real lives. Authenticity and transparency—not imagination and anonymity—became the cardinal rules of the blogosphere. Then came the rise of YouTube, the video sharing site, and social networking sites such as MySpace and Facebook. "Facebook became the first Web service that required accurate, validated identity, and that is what drove it to become the largest and fastest-growing platform of the cloud computing era," David Kirkpatrick, senior editor of *Fortune* magazine, observed.

Facebook became a game-changer, kicking off anyone who refused to use their real names. On Facebook and a new breed of copycat social networks, identity is front and center, grounded by real biographies, real friends and real media. On Twitter, the popular microblogging site, pictures (generally thumbnails of real people) accompany each member's tweet. Pseudonymity still has its place, but who you really are has become very important to anyone you want to do business with or socialize with. Many of us now spend most of our time online interacting with people in our social networks rather than with anonymous strangers on the Web.

Thus, identity in this context refers to characteristic features other people attribute to you as a result of your behaviors or Web presence. It is about how other people see you (if they can see you—otherwise it is just a persona), not how you see yourself.

But this is a fairly constricted view of identity, given the complex, dynamic ways we construct our own reality. "Both the birth of the social Web and security issues are forcing us to think about how to architect an identity layer that can scale to provide a lot of the essential things that we now expect of our online lives," Clippinger said. "The implications of this are quite enormous. I think getting identity right is essential to being able to scale the social Web."

Toward an open identity network

Looming just over the horizon is the third incarnation of online identity—call it identity in the cloud. Experts are at work trying to design a "user-centric open identity network," or a new "identity layer of the Web" that would give all of us the ability to manage, to some extent, our identities—that is, both our Web presence and offline identity. The idea is an identity system that is scalable (so it works everywhere), user-centric (serving your interests, instead of something done to you by outside interests) and, importantly, customizable. This new system would recognize that each of us has multiple identities. We will be able to spoon out bits and pieces of our identity, depending on the social or business context we find ourselves in.

> **An "intention economy" gives users control of their own attention and leads them to products, services, subjects and ideas that interest them.**

Doc Searls, a longtime promoter of digital identity who teaches at Harvard's Berkman Center for Internet & Society, believes such a system could supplant the advertising industry with an "intention economy" that gives users control of their own attention and leads them to products, services, subjects and ideas that interest them.[18]

Many of the discussions of identity, both online and offline, center on notions of privacy and security. But John Clippinger suggested that there are many ways to think about identity. One approach is to think of it as the ability to give the right people access to the right things at certain times, at certain locations, under certain circumstances.

In many situations, Clippinger said, an open identity network would authenticate only the information needed to complete a transaction, join an organization or interact with a government agency. The danger with divulging more information than necessary is that it can be aggregated by third parties and governments without an individual's knowledge or consent.

By using an open identity system, said Clippinger, "I may decide to reveal to you my age, my home address, proof that I'm over twenty-one and my bank account number. But you need not know other things about me, such as my interests or even my name, for me to obtain certain privileges or conduct a business transaction with you." This describes roughly how eBay works in serving as a trusted intermediary between a seller and buyer, either of whom may decide not to use their real names.

Creating a standard for identity in a cloud ecosystem allows us to think about how we want to parcel out identifying information about ourselves—how to fashion rules governing access to our personal information by people and institutions. Under such a scenario, if you wanted to rent a car from Avis, the identity system would vouch for your age, your car insurance and your driving record without having to reveal your name, address or social security number.

Anna Lysyanskaya, an associate professor of computer science at Brown University, told roundtable participants technology exists that would enable such a system, and she saw no conflict between outside reputation systems and a user-centric open identity system that gives users control over what information gets disclosed. In other words, a person should be able to remain completely anonymous in a private transaction. If something goes wrong after you have rented that car from Avis, an audit trail would exist that releases your name and other necessary information.

A central element of open identity is the notion of multiple identities. You could separate your identity into discrete units and assign different access permissions depending on your role in a given situation. You could create a business profile, a health care profile, a friend profile, a mom or singles profile, a virtual world profile, and so on. If all this sounds too complex for ordinary folks to handle, the experts have an answer for that, too: identity surrogates who would act on your behalf. Few identity software developers expect that most people will want to manage their own identities, Clippinger said, so the assumption is that an industry of "i-card" brokers will emerge that will compete to provide a rich choice of identity and privacy protection services. Such services might include dating, travel, music, sports, charitable investing, health care and civic, religious, cultural and political activities. "There are ways in which you can have an identity provider manage people's data without knowing who they are—now that's a trust proposition," said Clippinger.

Some surrogates may not even be human. Developers are crafting the next generation of bots and intelligent agents that can be released into the wild with knowledge of your tastes, preferences and needs. Whether operating on your mobile devices or housed in the cloud, software agents will automatically scan, negotiate, ferret out cool stuff, reveal identity information and act on our behalf in the next-generation Internet. This, too, is an important part of the identity layer: searches done for you instead of by you.

Where does the cloud come in? The identity layer resides not in a government or company database but in the cloud, so information storage can be fully distributed and supported by a variety of different, and potentially competing, companies and organizations. The cloud provides access to this new rich identity system—access by you to fix mistakes and manage certain facets of your personal history, and access by the rest of us to find out what we need to know about you to complete a transaction, let you join our organization, and so on. Because it would be adaptable to different circumstances, you could configure the system so that a hospital could access certain health records but not your financial records; a bank could access certain financial records but not your health records.

One way to think about the cloud is as "a mash-up of different kinds of social objects that form a consensus around certain governing information and exchange principles allowing people to create their own rules" for social and commercial interactions, Clippinger said.

This kind of approach is far different from the ill-fated plan put forward in 2000 and 2001 by Microsoft. Under the Passport plan, Microsoft would have been the trusted agent for all personal information and would have collected and stored data, such as credit card information, on the consumer's behalf. The goal was to make shopping at online retailers more convenient. But relatively few companies deployed Passport, and privacy advocates bristled at the technology. By 2004, Microsoft began to phase out the program.

Microsoft is now among the companies—along with IBM, Cisco, AMD, Intel, Oracle, GE and others—that have come to appreciate the magnitude of the change in the rules for global technology markets. "They came to recognize that they could not control it all—not their customers, suppliers, competition or the technology," Clippinger said. "For Microsoft and IBM, this represented a 180-degree change in their business strategies."

The course correction came about not because of a newfound altruism but because of the companies' recognition of a new kind of ecological capitalism, where their business interests were intertwined with the interests of customers, suppliers and even competitors. Competition has evolved beyond a multiplayer zero-sum game into a more complex, cooperative exchange where mutually advantageous outcomes depend on a new kind of rationality in a wider ecology of players.

Roundtable participant Kim Taipale, founder and executive director of the Center for Advanced Studies in Science and Technology, said the benefits of an open identity system for businesses were palpable. "One of the big costs in business is identifying who your customer is or who you are doing business with. Identity in the cloud removes some of the guesswork and reduces uncertainty in the reliance on a risk management process, bringing costs down."

One of the results of this more open business strategy has been the development of open source software for the new identity layer of the Internet. It recognizes that if a new identity infrastructure is to be accepted by citizens, banks, merchants and governments, it will have to be open and interoperable in order to be trusted. Even more remarkable, Clippinger said, is the agreement that the model for this open identity network must be user-centric, so control rests with individuals rather than governments or corporations.

That is not to say we will be able to devise our identities or rewrite our personal histories out of whole cloth. One of the challenges of any identity system is how to authenticate someone's real identity in a trusted way so third parties, such as merchants, will know you can pay your bills or you are old enough to make that credit card purchase. A secure identity system comes down to whom can I trust and who will trust me?

One approach to a secure identity system is coerced disclosure and authentication. Some people have proposed a national identity card, or a driver's license or social security card with mandatory biometric authentication such as fingerprints, facial recognition or retinal scans. Some European and Asian governments have already instituted national identity cards. But as Clippinger and others point out, hackers would easily compromise such a system while the rest of us would lose a measure of our civil liberties.

The alternative approach to coercive authentication is reflected in the design of an open identity system. Architecturally it would support the principles of equality of individual rights and provide for a highly decentralized and open governance model. Clippinger acknowledged that many aspects of the "accreditation problem" in such an authentication system remain to be resolved. "Are there going to be i-cards that will certify if someone is 18 or older, or cards that verify a certain income level? We don't know, but we do know that there will be a slew of services built on top of these certifications."

Microsoft, IBM, Novell and other companies plan to release their versions of the open identity system in mid- to late 2009, and Microsoft plans to release CardSpace,[19] an i-card service based on this open identity framework, in its newest Windows operating system.[20] If that happens it could rapidly become available on 300 to 400 million computers. If the system is adopted by the next generation of broadband wireless phones, then it could be available on more than one billion devices.

Separately, another consortium of companies is working together as part of the Information Card Foundation, a nonprofit organization dedicated to reducing the instance of identity theft by securing digital identities in place of traditional log-ons and passwords through an interoperable identity management system. Steering members of the foundation include representatives from Google, Microsoft, PayPal, Oracle, Novell and Equifax.[21]

Clippinger put forth a vision of individuals and businesses creating services on top of these identity platforms. People will be able to discover and construct their own social and commercial networks. They will be able to import and transfer their identities, relationships and personal information from one website to another without having to reenter personal information on each site or social network. Entrepreneurs and hobbyists will create markets for virtually anything: buyers and sellers of antiques, collectibles, housing, cars, food, sports equipment, video games, CDs. "What is now an impersonal experience on the Web will increasingly become more personal and contextual," Clippinger said. "People will know who you are, trade stories, recipes, tips and photos, and conduct business through the equivalent of a handshake."

In short, open identity would provide the foundation for people to invent and discover a new generation of social signals, advice services, affinity groups, organizations and eventually institutions. Because the identity layer is grounded on the principles of openness and equality, anyone would be able to create social networks, tagging systems, reputation systems or identity authentication systems. "Given the stakes involved," however, "don't expect this to happen without a titanic fight," Clippinger said.[22]

Marc Rotenberg, executive director of the Electronic Privacy Information Center [EPIC], agreed. "Institutions aren't going to be happy about this. They don't necessarily want people to move from how they've been characterized or understood in the past."

The dynamic nature of identity and privacy

Roundtable participants embraced the principles behind an open identity network. At the same time, several raised additional issues that need to be considered.

Mark Bregman, chief technology officer of Symantec, cautioned that systems or standards like the i-Card could fail to meet the fast-evolving precepts of the younger generation about issues of identity and privacy, and such systems may run into trouble in non-Western societies "where this idea of identity versus privacy, authority versus individual responsibility is vastly different than in our own."

Another consideration is the prospect that the open identity specification could give individuals a mechanism to manage their privacy. Some participants hoped that in the cloud would be an identity management system with a very strong potential for privacy enhancement inside authentication. Generally, the United States has relatively few guidelines governing the release of sensitive personal information. The Fair Credit Reporting Act, a federal law enacted in 1971, established a framework for collecting data about individuals who want to get credit, so that credit grantors could make evaluations of their creditworthiness. But few such frameworks exist in other areas, such as the health sector. If someone wants to get health insurance, an insurance company may want to find out if the applicant has a genetic marker for breast cancer. What should be the framework of rules and rights of the insured?

At the same time, participants wondered how interested Americans would be in managing their privacy: "Let's see if there's a marketplace for privacy. I would submit we have learned there is no marketplace for privacy. What drives people in their social intercourse, commerce and citizen interactions is convenience, not privacy. As the cloud emerges we're going to see some incredibly compelling and convenient applications, especially on mobile devices. But from what we've seen so far in the United States, we do not have a legal framework that in any way constrains what might be socially unacceptable exploitation of the convenience that the consumer wants. If you have a dispute with somebody over your privacy in the United States you have virtually no recourse."

> **"There would be no basis of trust in the absence of a secure flow of data."**
>
> *Marc Rotenberg*

Rotenberg, who has been waging privacy battles on Capitol Hill as head of EPIC, discussed privacy and identity as dynamic concepts. "The problem with privacy as a policy issue is that it's always been viewed as a very atomistic, individualistic value. The good thing about talking about identity and identity management is that it reminds us that we exist in a social context—that information flows between individuals and institutions, and that is the essential character of the modern discussion over information privacy. It's about these data flows and how we construct identity."

He recalled Tocqueville's observation about the unique character of Americans, particularly the power of voluntary association and the willingness of people to participate in community groups, religious groups and political groups. "Tocqueville observed that we were a highly dynamic society—that the American people were by nature constantly changing and reconstructing identity and moving among intermediate associations," Rotenberg said. "Americans were different from the aristocratic societies of Europe because of our fluid social mobility. Now I see the opportunity with identity management of carrying forward that same sense of mobility and dynamism that allows people and organizations and institutions to evolve."

The public often makes a number of false assumptions about privacy, Rotenberg said. First, privacy and data flows are not opposing values. In fact, as Europeans understand, the free flow of information is impossible without privacy protection. "In other words, if you could imagine a communication system where the communications were not secure, people would not be candid and open. So there would be no basis of trust in the absence of a secure flow of data."

Second, said Rotenberg, people often think of privacy as a static state when it is actually quite evolving and dynamic in modern culture. "Someone asked me, 'What are you doing on Facebook?' And, as a privacy advocate, I had to explain that it really is a marvelous paradox. The Facebook model is a very robust projection and assertion of persona to the world, and I think that's a good thing. It's characteristic of an open society that people are free to express their views on whatever they want. They may say brilliant things. They may say dumb things. They make those choices. We sort it out, and that's how we form social organization in an open society. And as we think about the new models and where identity fits in, I think it does come down to giving people a sense of control over shaping their own identity and a sense of trust in being able to participate in these new networks."

Self-identification vs. the power of the crowd

Jeffrey Dachis, chief executive officer in residence at Austin Ventures, observed that individuals will have only so much control in shaping public perceptions of their identity given the multitude of information sources about various aspects of their lives. "With the democratization of publishing tools out there, it doesn't really matter if I make an assertion about who I am if 100 other people are publishing things out on the Internet about me." To a large extent, we're evolving toward a world where you are who Google says you are. "The kind of tools and search capabilities available today in the cloud pose tremendous challenges to the filters we want to create for ourselves," said Dachis.

Those tools—search engine results, Facebook profiles, eBay seller ratings—are being manipulated every day, said Kim Taipale, founder and executive director of the Center for Advanced Studies in Science and Technology. An entire industry has sprung up around reputation management on Google. Taipale noted a parent at a New York City private school who had made his money in pornography: "He hired two PR firms that have now put up so many mundane, business-related posts about him all over the Web that the previous entries about porn are so far down the search results that nobody sees them. He looks like a completely different person."

Newspapers, too, are grappling with how to deal with identity and reputation in their digital archives. In August 2007, *The New York Times* public editor Clark Hoyt pointed to the case of Allen Kraus, a former deputy commissioner in the New York City Human Resources Administration who resigned his post 16 years earlier. Writes Hoyt, "If you look for him on Google, the first thing that pops up is not the home page of his consulting business. It's an old *New York Times* article: 'A Welfare Official Denies He Resigned Because of Inquiry.' "

To a large extent, we're evolving toward a world where you are who Google says you are.

Hoyt wrote that the *Times* editors "say they recognize that because the Internet has opened to the world material once available only from microfilm or musty clippings in the newspaper's library, they have a new obligation to minimize harm." Thus, they have agreed to open up their digital archives to correct even very old errors when a person can offer proof. But they have decided not to "sunset" negative pieces of information about individuals, and they are still mulling what else, if anything, they can do.[23]

Some digital sleight-of-hand is already taking place online. Marc Rotenberg related the social experiment in which a small group created a false identity on Facebook—"an unreal human"—and within a day managed to get a large number of people to "friend" him. "So there's a real question there of whether that's really a valid identity or not," and whether other Facebook members are making equally specious identity claims, said Rotenberg.

But David Kirkpatrick, senior editor of Internet and technology at *Fortune* Magazine, responded that a false identity on a site like Facebook has inherent limitations. "The kind of impact you can have with a false identity is much more constricted than what you would be able to do with an identity that was real and validated by others who knew you."

J.D. Lasica, president of Socialmedia.biz, added that while some aspects of online identity can be manipulated, and individuals can configure their identities in their Facebook and LinkedIn profiles, other aspects of online identities fall outside their control. People now discover images and videos of ourselves on image sharing and video sharing sites, tagged with their names by friends, foes and strangers. This cloud of identity will grow exponentially over time, so that a person who cannot be found through Google image search will be the exception rather than the rule. Those who may not care to reveal their age may find themselves the subject of a Wikipedia entry where it is not easy to scrub out a birth date.

Secrets are harder to keep today. "[Sun Microsystems CEO] Scott McNealy made a mistake when he said privacy is dead," Taipale said. "He should have said secrecy is dead. The information exists out there somewhere. It's no longer possible to keep secrets. The question is, how does information—or how should information—get used?"

Mark Bregman, chief technology officer of Symantec, observed that our identities are becoming increasingly digital, from banking and government service to purchasing consumer goods to finding a job to organizing a fund-raising campaign for a charitable cause. The social Web is accelerating that trend and preserving our digital footprints with perfect fidelity. "That's a fundamental change between our traditional notion of identity and digital identity, and it's something that we have to figure out how to solve," he said.

This lurch toward the social Web is taking place at a rapid pace in the United States, but Arturo Artom, CEO of Milan-based *Your Truman Show*, said the uptake has been slower in Europe and other parts of the world. While ninety-five percent of the roundtable participants had active Facebook profiles, only ten to twenty-five percent of an equivalent gathering in Europe would typically have Facebook accounts, Artom said. "Facebook is something that is quite scary from a European point of view," he noted.

But David Kirkpatrick, who is writing a book about Facebook, said the service is doubling its membership in most European countries roughly every six months and should catch up to the penetration rate in the United States in due time. While press attention has focused on Facebook's halting steps to turn members into marketers hawking their favorite products through its Beacon program, an equally interesting dimension is "how Facebook demonstrates that people rely on identity for their socializing," Kirkpatrick said. "It's all about identity."

Lucio Stanca, a member of the Italian Parliament, told the roundtable that identity, security and privacy are interconnected values, and governments and the private sector must devise policies that address fast-changing cultural norms. "A few days ago I came to this country and Customs asked me for fingerprint identity. Five years ago this was inconceivable because this was a violation of my personal privacy, but today I accept the tradeoff because I also want to be secure. As we move toward the cloud, these rules and policies will become more complex. I don't know how you can manage identity, security and privacy on a global scale in a way that can just be user-centric. Those cannot be just left to the market."

New Concepts of Money

In 1989, Walter Wriston, former chief executive officer of Citicorp, suggested that society is moving currency from the gold standard to the information standard. That prophesy is largely true today, but in the future world of commoditized computing and machines reading machines, information could actually replace money for many purposes.

Already we see the concept of money changing, as instant global communications make possible bartering not only for tangible goods but also for text minutes, airline miles, virtual world currency and other non-physical assets. The implications loom large as the changing nature of identity influences new currencies and vice versa.

Paul Romer, a professor at the Graduate School of Business at Stanford University, played the role of myth buster in knocking down one of the most widely assumed falsehoods of the information economy: that society is heading to an economy where electronic currency will replace cold, hard cash. In truth, real currency—the bills people carry in their wallets and stash in their bedroom hiding spots—has doubled from 1965 to 2005 and now amounts to about $2,500 per person on average.

"The people who say that currency is going away or the government won't have any control over the economy because currency is disappearing—the data don't support that assertion," Romer said. "Real currency per capita has been growing and it's been growing more rapidly recently." Convenience and anonymity are two factors spurring that growth.

While it is often assumed that electronic currency presents more privacy issues than traditional currency, Brown University professor Anna Lysyanskaya argued that privacy-preserving safeguards could be implemented that include encryption and other methods that tie funds to an account with the account holder's need to reveal his or her identity. "There is not necessarily a conflict between privacy and online payment systems," she said.

Money has several different purposes in our society, observed Esther Dyson, chairman of EDventure Holdings. It is a mechanism that allows people to exchange goods and services, but it is also a measure of value. Gold and diamonds have no intrinsic worth, but they are imbued with value by society.

New measurements of value

In the new economy, new measurements of social value have come into being, such as a company's or person's carbon footprint, or a player's accumulation of virtual goods in an online game community like World of Warcraft. Susan Wu, a principal with Charles River Ventures, points out that people spend more than $1.5 billion a year on virtual items such as pets, coins, avatars and bling.[24] While these virtual objects are nothing more than a series of digital 1s and 0s stored on a remote database, we accord them an intrinsic value that translates into real-world monetary exchanges in online marketplaces. In the virtual world Second Life, members buy and sell virtual objects with Linden dollars, and you can buy or sell Linden dollars for real dollars. The exchange rate at the Linden Dollar Exchange is constantly changing but is generally between 260 and 300 Linden dollars for one U.S. dollar.[25]

More and more, however, people are coming to place greater value on time, attention from others and other attributes that enhance their personal capabilities and help them control their online (and occasionally offline) lives. Some people want productivity; others want fun. Some want recognition; others want privacy. (The attention—or recognition—individuals crave from and bestow on others in the "attention economy" is very different from the "attention" focused on by marketers interested only in consumers' propensity to buy the products they pay attention to, Esther Dyson noted.) To cite one example, Dyson pointed to a Silicon Valley startup called Skydeck, which helps people keep track of their cell phone calls and text messages in a way that enables them to gain value beyond monitoring their bills: you can tell who you are talking with the most, who is running up your bills, how long it has been since you last spoke. To some extent, Skydeck can map your true social network and help you manage your attention to others.

Identity and direct ties are even more intrinsic to 23andMe, a genetics service where Dyson is a board member. By paying $399 and submitting a swab of saliva to the company's (outsourced) lab, a person receives a breakdown of his or her genome, data on their tendencies for more than ninety traits and diseases, and options for comparing their data with those of friends and relatives. "See your personal history through a new lens with high-resolution maternal and paternal lineage, ancestry painting, and similarity to various global populations," the site promises. Members can use the site to share data with family members or strangers to "see what you have in common and what makes you unique!" [26]

> **In the digital economy, money is not the only currency; value—in the form of reputation, status, attention or information— is another.**
>
> *Esther Dyson and Paul Romer*

In the digital economy, Romer and Dyson pointed out, money is not the only currency; value—in the form of reputation, status, attention or information—is another. eBay accords sellers and buyers reputation points based on how well a transaction goes. RentACoder provides clients with programmers' track records and work histories. Facebook and LinkedIn provide credibility to users based on their number of friends or connections. Flickr tells you how many people are viewing your photos, and Google Analytics provide up-to-the-minute statistics on how many people are viewing your site, where they come from and how they arrived there.

Said Romer, "I bet if there isn't already there will soon be somebody who will charge you a certain price to give you a certain number of additional friends on Facebook. So if you want to have more friends or high-value friends, somebody will set up a business that for dollars you can buy friends. The more friends you have, the more value you're accorded."

Kim Taipale of the Center for Advanced Studies in Science and Technology, drew a parallel to an existing old media model: the celebrity market. "When we do brand analysis we look at how many mentions of the celebrity appear in *People* magazine or the *Hollywood Reporter* or the trade journals, and those mentions translate directly into dollars: 'x' number of mentions correlates to 'x' number of dollars in licensing fees." The point, he said, is that when your social capital gets large enough, you will be able to find ways to monetize it.

J.D. Lasica, president of socialmedia.biz, observed that the vast majority of people writing on seventy million blogs are doing so not to attract advertising income but to enhance their reputations. "Today, for a social media consultant or a public relations specialist or someone who's starting out in journalism, if you don't have a blog it's considered something of a black mark," he said.

Indeed, we ascribe value to many things besides money or things. We use a certain credit card to rack up frequent flyer miles on our favorite air-line. We enroll in rewards programs that funnel a portion of purchases made toward nonprofits or charitable causes. "I think the ability to exper-iment in the cloud will put more of these kinds of experiments into play," said John Clippinger of the Berkman Center for Internet and Society.

Lasica pointed to examples of online reputation translating into real-world currency through grassroots exchange networks. On the nonprofit site *Kiva.org*, entrepreneurs in the developing world put their biogra-phies and business plans onto the site, and people from around the globe put up real cash (generally $25 microloans) to serve as business loans for each project. As in many Web 2.0 sites, the lender directs his money toward a specific person. The site then facilitates the loan—accepting donations but charging nothing for the transaction—and tracks the pro-ject until repayment is made. The site says ninety-five percent of all loans—a total of more than $25 million—have been repaid.[27]

Metrics around attention and reputation

Now that attention and reputation are becoming somewhat mea-sureable through factors such as the number of friends you have on Facebook or the number of followers on Twitter, you can take steps to move up the power curve by translating those metrics into real dollars or by parlaying or bartering your high-profile status into access to peo-ple, power or parties.

With currency, Marc Rotenberg, executive director of Electronic Privacy Information Center, observed, we have a common frame of reference: the monetary unit. But in an age where identity increasingly looms large, different factors come into play. What value do you accrue by attaching your endorsement or brand to my Web page or blog? What kind of information attached to your identity do you want to share?

Hal Varian, chief economist of Google, staked out an opposing view from other participants on the issue of reputation as a form of currency. "I don't think it's a good idea to think of it as a currency. It's really an asset that you can trade for money or for other considerations, and of course if you're an eBay merchant and you sell your business to someone and they keep the same name and email address, your reputation goes right along with the business, just like any other fiscal business, so there's nothing mysterious in that sense."

It is tricky to build a website reputation engine that cannot be gamed. Varian pointed to some of the widely discussed shortcomings of the eBay ratings system. Ratings are generally very high because a merchant with a lower rating just rejoins under a different identity and starts over. Reminders to rate the merchant are initiated by the merchant, but he does so only if the transaction went well. Groups of merchants have formed coalitions to puff up each other's reputations by "selling" items and trading high ratings even if no goods are actually exchanged.

Max Mancini, senior director of mobile, platform and disruptive innovation at eBay, said the company implemented a major policy change in mid-2008 to address some of those concerns. eBay no longer allows sellers to give negative feedback to buyers because of the gaming that took place with sellers "essentially extorting" 100 percent satisfaction marks from buyers in some cases. In place of the bidirectional public mechanism for reputation and feedback, eBay now allows sellers to take action against buyers who behave with bad intent, but not in a public forum.

Brad Johnson, principal of McKinsey & Company, told the roundtable that the full effects of identity and reputation systems have yet to be realized. "Maybe we're in early days and actually there will be a new class of money, a new set of things of value that we can draw upon that never link to actual dollars. If the kind and number of currencies proliferate, I wonder if that leads to a lot of complexity that overwhelms the potential productivity gains of this."

Around the globe, what amounts to alternative currency systems have sprung up. Said Michael DeNoma, group executive director of consumer banking at Standard Chartered PLC, "In the developing world, the transaction cost around currency is extremely expensive, not only for the financial institution but for the individual. So people have begun to route around the banking system. What has happened globally is that with mobile phones there has been a revolution in turning currency into digital money, in effect, and this happened in particular in India and China where there are massive distribution networks that sell minutes for cash. They'll sell it down to the equivalent of five cents worth of minutes, and the air time increasingly becomes a settlement currency in and of itself. Now that is a hugely powerful development. In China you can buy movie tickets with your air time. So what's happened, interestingly, is the mobile phone companies, by putting up this reselling of the minutes driven by an industry moving to prepaid and not billed, has an inability to collect generally, so outside the U.S. virtually everything is prepaid."

William Coleman of Cassatt Corporation took the discussion about money and value a step into the future by envisioning the prospect of societies turned upside down by what is coming in quantum material sciences when we might be able to produce anything imaginable from the most basic elements. "In the information age, the lingua franca of the world is intellectual property. With the coming advent of nanotechnologies that makes intellectual property transportable and reproducible—not in digital form but in real-world physical form—then creating a bartered market for the exchange of intellectual capital is something that will happen. What happens when the value of materials goes to zero? How will taxing property or material goods work in such a world? How will it affect our ability to fund schools, roads and local services? We are just at the beginning of an escalating slope of change that will affect how we interact socially, culturally, politically."

Implications for Commerce

The rise of the cloud may well foretell dramatic shifts in the commercial sector. No longer do start-ups need to raise hundreds of thousands of dollars in angel seed funding to acquire the servers and technical infrastructure it takes to get a business off the ground. As cloud platforms become accessible to anyone with an Internet connection, entrepreneurs with a better idea or service will attain instant global reach for even the smallest niche product or service. A new generation of systems will arise for barter, escrow, authentication and authorization. Potentially this will lead to lower costs for products and services as well as greater customer convenience in pulling what we want when we want it. Yet the same trends could very well lead to greater volatility and disruption, destabilizing industries and market leaders and over-rewarding winners.

The roundtable took up such questions as how might consumers benefit or lose from these trends. What are the implications for transaction- and location-based businesses? Will large companies or small start-ups make the first push into business-to-consumer cloud commerce? How do these trends affect risk-taking by businesses and individuals?

Society will not see a big bang where cloud-enabled companies appear overnight and commerce suddenly looks very different, principal of McKinsey and Company, Inc., Brad Johnson, told the roundtable participants. "I think we're going to see an evolutionary path over the next twenty to thirty years as social mores continue to change, as the reach of IT continues to increase and as costs increasingly become lower."

The shift toward cloud services and the cloud as a platform will be an evolutionary one, a process in which the cloud itself disappears into the background as it becomes just an unspoken part of the way things are. Johnson drew a parallel to society's changing attitudes toward online dating and social media, two early manifestations of distributed remote communities (and precursors to cloud computing). Ten to fifteen years ago the idea of finding a partner or mate on the Web struck many people as unusual, while today singles take online dating services as part of the terrain. Young people reveal hugely personal details about themselves on Facebook and MySpace. Similarly, the idea that millions of people would contribute time and energy for free to an online knowledge base called Wikipedia would have struck many as farfetched just a few years ago. But the culture has moved toward a more engaged, participative citizenry in a real and long-lasting way.

The cloud will lower costs per use of whatever IT asset a company uses—not just storage but also bandwidth or computation. For many large companies, these cost savings will be years away as the costs involved in switching over from legacy systems does not yet justify a leap to the cloud. For nimbler small or mid-size businesses, infrastructure and efficiency cost savings will be more immediate.

"Overall, I think that the theme here is greater competitive intensity," Johnson said. "Depending on your perspective, that's either an unmitigated good, or if you're an incumbent firm with a great market share, greater competitive intensity may not be so desirable. In general, competitive intensity leads to productivity gains, and these gains matter because they contribute to quality of life. Productivity gains lead to better health care access, better educational access—it really does matter to individuals. It's also going to lead to tremendous managerial innovation that will in turn drive additional productivity gains. For the consumer, greater competitive intensity almost always leads to greater choice and lower prices."

Twelve features of the cloud economy

With Johnson leading the way, the roundtable identified twelve ways the cloud will transform business:

1. Greater global reach

2. Greater customization

3. Reduced barriers to entry

4. The end of scale

5. Easier entry into adjacent markets

6. Greater specialization

7. Greater innovation and experimentation

8. Greater information transparency

9. Greater organizational complexity

10. Faster turnaround times and greater speed to market

11. Greater competitive intensity and disruption of existing markets

12. A shift from marketing push to customer pull.

Greater global reach. In the nineteenth century, Western businessmen fantasized about opening up China's markets, with tens of millions of

Chinese clamoring for Western goods. By and large, that dream never materialized. But the Internet and the advent of the cloud raise the prospect that traditional barriers—national borders, differences in language and culture—no longer present insuperable obstacles. In a very real sense, people and firms are now "born global." Digital goods and physical goods now flow freely from the developing world to the West and vice versa. There are exceptions. For example, Amazon.com customers in the United Kingdom or France cannot purchase new releases of American movies until they open in each country's domestic market many months later. On the whole, however, it has never been easier to hang one's shingle and proclaim "open for business" to the global marketplace.

The new economics of the Internet enables new companies to create near instant global footprints, with potentially seismic shifts in market share and profitability of vertical markets over the long term as new entrants elbow their way to the front of the pack on the basis of greater customization or specialization, more innovative products and lower costs.

"This is the first market in the history of the world where there are no borders—period," William Coleman said. "I can buy from anybody on the globe on the fly if they have what I want, they have a reputable identity and they're connected by an IP [Internet Protocol] address. This is the ultimate level of transparency. It puts competition into the stratosphere."

Loncin, a professional motorcycle parts exporter in southwest China, has created a virtual supply chain of manufacturers and suppliers to assemble motorcycles for export to local markets in East Asia. The company, with nearly 10,000 employees, also exports all-terrain vehicles and scooters to 80 countries.

Li & Fung, a company based in Hong Kong, has assembled a global process network of nearly 10,000 business partners in the clothing industry. It uses the network to put together customized supply chains for clothes designers.[28]

Daniel Burton of Salesforce.com said the big promise of the cloud is not just as a development platform—many software coders have used Amazon's cloud services to develop beta sites—but as an end-to-end business platform. "Today you can run your entire business on the cloud," he said. The cloud platform and cloud services offered by companies like Salesforce.com already enable a much wider swath of small businesses to tap into the global marketplace, but the phenomenon is only beginning.

Burton painted a picture of how a new small business might take advantage of new global opportunities: "If I'm an entrepreneur in Varanasi, India, and I don't have much cash and I don't have a distribution system and I don't have contracts and I don't have a payment system, I can go onto a site like Salesforce.com, I can build an application from scratch through a Web browser. I can post that on Salesforce. I then have an immediate global distribution system so that everybody coming to that Salesforce platform can see this application and an online sales form and a credit card payment system for customers. Suddenly, for a fraction of the cost, a developer anywhere in the world can not only come up with a great idea, they can create a product. They can post it on an international marketing distribution system, and they can collect all the payments for it. We haven't even begun to see the possibilities of where this is going."

Greater customization. While the Long Tail [a phrase coined to describe the niche strategy of businesses] has been somewhat overhyped, its impact on commerce has been unmistakable. Niche is the coin of the realm in the Long Tail. The cloud takes the Long Tail and enables the production of niche products and customized services that would not have been possible without an inexpensive virtual supply chain.

Websites that enable users to offer product reviews or custom-order a product with microprecision have been around for years. But a new breed of e-commerce is emerging that allows users to actually design the products themselves. For example, on the website *Threadless.com,* a downloadable digital toolkit lets members submit designs for T-shirts, wall prints and other merchandise. Fellow members then comment and vote on the best designs; winners receive anywhere from $2,500 to $10,000, and customers can purchase items that are produced in bulk. Nearly all of the transactions take place on the site. Unlike big-box retailers, the company's website says, "our product line changes every week and most retailers are not equipped to handle change that fast."[29] Such an approach enables a tremendous proliferation in consumer choice because consumers themselves are specifying the products.

Technology and the Internet are swallowing those products that can become digital—music, movies and books—while digitizing the operations of those that cannot, Johnson said. The effect of this trend toward digitization and customization has been to broaden the global reach of companies, while enabling them to concentrate on ever-finer slices of that global market—a kind of global pooling of micromarket demand. Indeed, Threadless can afford to sell hundreds more varieties of T-shirts than any physical retailer could stock profitably. Other online retailers are pursuing a DIY business model: *ChoiceShirts.com* lets customers design their own T-shirts. *Makeyourownjeans.com* lets customers order tailor-made blue jeans, pant suits, shirts and suits. Meanwhile, a hobbyist obsessed with building 1/48th scale radio-controlled battleships can make a living from his passion, by seeking out all his fellow hobbyists around the world on the Internet.

Customization in the cloud does not benefit only niche players. The big-box retailers are also finding opportunities for segmentation and targeting in the cloud. With much larger numbers of customers visiting their websites than could ever walk through the doors of a store, retailers such as Old Navy and the Gap are undertaking their own modernization efforts by targeting customers who do not fit standard retail profiles, such as those who do not like to shop in stores or who are constantly frustrated because they do not fit into standard sizes. If these customer segments do not overlap with existing segments, all the better. They represent new market share and new profits. Already, forty percent of Lands' End jeans and trouser sales are customized online, where customers can tailor their clothing fit with precision.

Reduced barriers to entry. New technologies and the Internet make it easier than ever for new competitors to enter the market anywhere in the world. The cloud extends those capabilities. A ten-person company can be "born global" as a multinational operation with a global market presence, dramatically lowering the barriers to entry in many established markets. Much more than outsourcing, the born-global concept is causing companies to rethink the locus of decision-making, innovation and their role in the industry value chain.

Max Mancini of eBay argued that small businesses and entrepreneurs will take advantage of cloud technologies to provide cloud services that create value for customers by building on top of existing services or applications. Mash-ups will likely be an important part of this phenomenon, he said. In an application mash-up, developers take an application like Google Maps and add a dataset on top of it to chart things like houses for sale or rent (*http://housingmaps.com*) or crimes that take place in a specific neighborhood (*http://chicago.everyblock.com/crime/*).

"I think the real innovation is not going to come out of the large companies," Mancini said. "Corporations will create the infrastructures and they'll help accelerate the cloud, but ultimately what's going to enable it are the people who create these mash-ups and the smaller developers who now have a lower barrier to entry."

The end of scale. Certainly, mass production to drive down costs still matters in a world where economies of scale put everything from television sets to iPhones to watches within reach of the average person's pocketbook. The notion here is not that scale no longer matters but that it is no longer an integral pillar of the new economy. For an increasing number of industries, the benefits of scope will far outweigh the traditional benefits of scale. Threadless is instructive here as well. The company has very few employees. Its business model is based upon the hundreds of thousands of participants who enjoy designing the products. Threadless's physical footprint is quite minimal: the company has only one physical retail store (in Chicago), while the vast majority of its sales are done online. Its shirts are manufactured by a contract manufacturer somewhere, but the company has crowdsourced all design resources to its customers.

> **For an increasing number of industries, the benefits of scope will far outweigh the traditional benefits of scale.**

Traditionally, companies focused on a particular market and exploited it before thinking about others. They did not contemplate entering new markets until they had the resources and scale to go through the expensive and time-consuming process of establishing a presence in the new market and slowly building market share. Technology allows companies to establish a global presence at a reasonable scale. By piggybacking on standardized technology infrastructures like the cloud and using new software tools for coordinating operations, companies can quickly set up a credible online presence in foreign markets.

Easier entry into adjacent markets. The traditional borders between vertical markets have begun to crumble. Businesses now have an increased ability to enter adjacent markets because of the ability of the cloud to circumvent or break down traditional regulatory and other barriers to free trade and exchange. For example, Japanese wireless providers have built payment systems that are taking business away from banks and credit cards. As a result, the Japanese are increasingly turning to the wireless providers as their preferred method of paying for things. At grocery stores, shoppers can easily swipe a cell phone containing currency units, hooked up to a network terminal at the checkout stand for instant payment. The system makes checkouts faster and more convenient, in turn increasing sales while lowering costs. Meanwhile, search engine companies like Google and Yahoo have entered the online advertising business and now dominate the space. Incumbent advertising networks in the traditional media are scrambling to keep up, while advertisers have begun to abandon newspapers in favor of new media markets.

Greater specialization. Historically people have had one employer at a time where they generally performed a small number of similar tasks every day. You worked for one company, not a dozen. As a result, your ability to learn a specialty or a narrow set of skills was limited by the extent to which your company had a market for your capability. As the cloud continues to emerge and as connectivity becomes ubiquitous and cheap, you see people contributing in very narrow, specialized ways across a range of markets. For example, a top coder might delve into the specific subsets of a computer science problem. A professional might devote just a fraction of her time to some very specialized task. The ability to take employees from "units of one" to "fractions" will lead to tremendously greater specialization, which in the end results in a net positive for commerce, product development, productivity and the economy. If done correctly, the employee will achieve greater job satisfaction as she expands her skill set.

One of the advantages of applying technology to interactive work is that the work can be broken up into highly specialized pieces while maintaining some degree of coordination, Brad Johnson said. The work does not need to be done by the company's employees. For certain tasks, such as computer programming, websites like TopCoder enable companies to post difficult programming challenges to a global community of programmers who like to show off their prowess to a large audience. Rather than being confined to a limited talent pool, companies can get this complex work done more cheaply and often more effectively because they can open it up to a global labor pool where talent is deeper and costs are lower. Companies no longer pay for employees; they pay for solutions, essentially fractionalizing the employee into ever smaller and more productive slices of labor by enabling co-location in a virtual way through technology.

In the cloud economy, products become projects. Technology enables companies to build and tear apart alliances and partnerships on an as-needed basis. Product decisions are becoming less dependent upon a fixed list of suppliers than on the range of suppliers available. Relationships come together based on a particular product or project and then disband at the end.

In the cloud economy, products become projects.

The beginnings of this move toward specialization is already on display in certain global supply chains, where workers in disparate venues focus on one aspect of the manufacturing process. For instance, eighteen different companies were involved in developing and manufacturing the first Apple iPod. Though it is called an Apple product, it actually is a mélange of foreign components and inputs all packaged together with expert design, marketing and a globally recognized brand image. While Apple outlined the general design of the iPod, a company called Portal Player built it, farming out manufacturing tasks to a variety of local ecosystems: the screen came from Japan, digital to analog conversion came from Scotland, the CPU came from the United Kingdom, software came from India and power management came from Silicon Valley, according to John Seely Brown, independent co-chair of the Deloitte Center for Edge Innovation. "PortalPlayer finds these incredible local world-class specializations and then they use the Net to interconnect everything together," he said.

Andrew Leonard wrote in *Salon*:

> Crack open an iPod and what do you see? Laid out in silicon is a road map for the world economy: globalized, outsourced, offshored, interconnected and complex. Take a look at the components: the hard drive, circuit board, click wheel, battery pack and all the rest. The iPod is a striking Apple success story, but the first thing worth noting is that Apple doesn't "make" it.

Steve Jobs and Co. led the overall design, but the pieces get put together in China by a pair of Taiwanese firms.

But let's go deeper, into the brains of the iPod, the microchip that makes the music player go. Designed by a Silicon Valley company called PortalPlayer, this "controller" chip offers the real blueprint of how the modern world works. Headquartered in the U.S., PortalPlayer got its chip into one of the world's most coveted consumer electronic devices by outsourcing or subcontracting every possible step of design and manufacturing. By operating around the clock, with teams of engineers across the globe hammering out the chip's hardware design and essential software, PortalPlayer relentlessly delivered new versions of the chip, each one cheaper and faster than the one before, packed with more features but using less power.[30]

Specialization is not just for multinational corporations. "With the cloud," Brown told the roundtable, "startups are beginning to attack problems that were basically unthinkable a few years ago. If a small startup needs $1 million for an electron microscope, that's not going to fly. But now they can reach out and grab one online, and that's happening time and time again."

Nanostellar, a small "nano" or material sciences company that Brown advises, is building a precious material for catalytic converters that would dramatically reduce the price of those converters around the world. "You could not have taken this to a national lab five years ago and gotten them to work on it. It's too complicated. But this whole thing is being done in a garage—a sizable garage, but still a garage." And the game is not only having everything done on cluster computing in terms of all the quantum mechanical calculations and multi-scale analysis, but then each night, when they construct a particle, they ship it out to an electron microscope on the Net, do the experiments at night time, and then get the results back in the morning for updating their simulation models. So working in the cloud is not just computation, but the ability to have incredible instrumentation attached.

Brown added, "The cloud and optical communication makes us think the world is flat, but in fact the world is becoming spikier than ever. These little tiny local ecosystems have really increased radical specialization."

Greater innovation and experimentation. Much of the business community's thinking in the 20th century was informed by the notion of scalable efficiencies. What is emerging in the new century is the idea of "scalable learning," with small, independent operations leveraging each other's innovations and building on top of the business culture. "The amount of learning that happens by connecting these incredible spikes together is tremendous, and so our ability to learn faster by working with one another is really driving the pace of innovation that we see happening," Brown said.

What is emerging in the new century is the idea of "scalable learning."

Hal Varian of Google said the cloud enables entrepreneurs and IT managers to use "combinatorial innovation" to cheaply try new combinations of technology, discard those that do not work and move on to new models.

Varian pointed to the first automobile assembly lines, which Henry Ford built in 1909, as models of continual experimentation. Today, innovation is harder to come by in Detroit, while Toyota has pioneered a culture of reinvention and risk-taking that Silicon Valley would recognize.

"Toyota has a robust production system: you hypothesize, you implement, you test, you measure and you reflect—in that cycle," Brown said. That approach seems to be a hallmark of the cloud economy. With a startup like Nanostellar, he said, "the number of microexperiments being run day in and day out is really astounding, because you can look at today's data, you can build a hypothesis and you can test on tomorrow's real data. That cycle is happening in the flexibility of the cloud, but also in the ways that these service companies are really looking at this thing, and I think we're going to see those who are leaders in the game drive this cycle of constant experimentation, and they're going to create a competitive edge. It's going to be very hard to catch up, as we're finding out with Toyota."

Varian agreed and pointed to the culture of innovation that Google tries to nurture. "One thing that is enabled by cloud computing, which

I think is not sufficiently appreciated, is this idea of continuous product improvement," he said. "At Google, at any one time we're running over 400 experiments on the search algorithm and on the ads algorithm to improve the look and feel of our offerings. Many of these experiments are very, very small, shifting page elements along to the right, changing a color, changing a font. Others will be changes in the underlying algorithm. They're carefully designed experiments with treatment, control, varying sample sizes—there's a whole process of rolling out changes and seeing what the impact is. This allows us to continually evolve the product. So any time you search on Google the odds are very high that you're in at least one experiment and perhaps four or five different experiments. You can do this with any product that you're developing.

"We're doing the same thing with Google Apps, although there the experimental group is us—we're using Google Apps inside of the organization and most of the larger changes occur first internally before they are made available to the users." Google Apps, frequently held up as an early model of cloud computing, lets users store and share Word documents, spreadsheets and other applications on Google's servers for ready access by anyone with the proper password. A copy of your files is stored in the cloud, you can restore any version you want, and you can synchronize with an offline activity. "The really, really big component that's valuable to the user is this collaboration aspect," Varian said, citing software companies that tackle projects with five- to ten-person teams. "What most people do now is send around these doc files with track changes, and there are sixty different versions of the PowerPoint presentation, and people are commenting on it and integrating it. It's a whole bunch of silly make-work because what you want to do is make that collaboration transparent and have a multi-authored document from beginning to end. We've been using them internally and, believe me, once you shift the organization over to using that model for multi-authored documents, you will never go back to the old model, because it's just so much easier."

Greater information transparency. The distributed, borderless nature of the cloud leads inevitably to global reach, global penetration and global information sharing. Traditional marketing will not disappear, but rising up alongside it will be an information ecosystem built on transparency and participatory media that enables consumers to tap into a knowledge base about what to buy, who to buy it from, how much to pay for it, how to use it and so on. Many companies and business models today rely on information opacity. That is especially evident in the travel and hotel industries, where information transparency is significantly driving down prices. Every time you research a travel destination before making a reservation, you are taking part in this process. More companies will emerge with a business model of aggregating, synthesizing and distributing useful, vetted information about consumer products and services.

The Internet makes it easier for consumers to compare offerings online, which increases price pressures on providers. Yet by diversifying their offerings online, McKinsey & Company's Brad Johnson said, traditional providers can take the edge off this pressure. For example, the clothing retailer Gap claims more than $500 million in sales from its website, which offers more sizes and colors than can be kept in the inventories of its many retail outlets.

Greater organizational complexity. Many decades ago hierarchical organizations arose, at least in part, because they satisfied a basic human desire: the need for order. Someone was the boss. Managers controlled the movements of their direct reports like pieces on a chessboard. Today's emergent organizations—called "starfish organizations" by roundtable member Rod Beckstrom in his book "The Spider and the Starfish"—often take a more distributed, collaborative approach to solving problems and managing tasks. A traditional command and control decision-making process is becoming a foreign notion to many of today's high-skilled workers. To be sure, creating a nonhierarchical business division or using "fractional employees" to dole out dozens of specialized tasks may be productive and make strategic sense, but it is also a more complex proposition. How do you coordinate all of these moving parts in an intelligent way?

Technology enables companies to have larger footprints with fewer people, but this also introduces challenges for maintaining productive communication and collaboration across dispersed locations. Interactive work is the fastest growing portion of the global labor economy. But it is difficult to develop a new product or create a marketing campaign in an automated or rules-based fashion. If this kind of work is going to take advantage of the true benefits of globalization, such as access to a broader, deeper, more talented and less expensive workforce, coordination mechanisms are needed.

Companies are actively struggling to reduce the coordination costs of going global. There are two principal ways to do this today:

- *Consolidate.* To the extent that multiple websites or other communication channels are being used to coordinate an activity, such as product development, companies are trying to aggregate users of different channels together. Thus, instead of trying to coordinate product development across ten different websites, put them together on one website.

- *Self-manage.* One of the reasons online communities like eBay have become so successful is that they have clear, simple rules for engagement and conduct that make them essentially self-managing. Through mechanisms like peer review, user support forums and problem reporting, companies do not need to expend as much energy and resources as they would if they tried to manage these communities directly.

Learning to manage a global operation efficiently and effectively will be an even more important competitive weapon in the future. Whether a workforce has five or 50,000 employees, mastering the complexities of a global workforce will be one of the challenges of the cloud economy.

Faster turnaround times and greater speed to market. Esther Dyson of EDventure Holdings pointed out the dramatic change in scale in how time is used and viewed in the new economy. "Things move much faster today. Things get started much faster. They die much faster." This trend is accelerating. The speed of everything is increasing dramatically, and this has an impact on multiple levels: in the insurance and real estate sectors, where underwriting departments are bumping up against the realities of a mobile, short-term work force, in investment circles, where a company's management team may prove more important than how much money it generates today (as long as the investors are in it for the long term). Dyson added, "This creates a challenge for long-term investing in general, and for public policy as well. Just as investors are driven by short-term returns, politicians and officals are often driven by polls and elections—to say nothing of the exigencies of fund-raising.

Will the new technologies drive us toward an accelerated evolutionary system where bad businesses disappear and only good businesses remain? One good thing about evolution is that it usually operates fairly slowly and allows for a lot of variation."

Technology increases transparency and integration across a supply chain, which can reduce time to market and decrease inventory levels and costs. Wal-Mart offers the most famous example of using this technology capability to create competitive advantage. Wal-Mart's IT systems have continuously improved productivity by providing visibility into their supply chain, optimizing the flow of goods to maximize in-store labor efficiency, using forecasting tools to align staffing levels with needs and other methods that have allowed the company to offer lower prices and in turn create a virtuous cycle as their increased scale allows them to press suppliers for better prices, which in turn can be passed on (completely or in part) to consumers.

Greater competitive intensity and disruption of existing markets. New technologies and the Internet are bringing new competitive intensities to business on multiple fronts, creating the potential for dramatic shifts in profits and value across industries. For existing companies—and especially for new ones—these new forces enable the creation of instant global operations and customer bases. This is especially true if the products are digital or heavily information based. Through the use of technology and the Internet, distribution costs for information-based products are near zero, and the costs of making additional products are minimal. Yet even makers of physical products can afford to fragment their operations and place them in whatever location makes the most economic and business sense—marketing in California, software development in the Ukraine, manufacturing in China—while using technology as an inexpensive glue for coordination. Clearly, technology has already had a major impact on competitive intensity across industries and markets. As technology continues to improve, competitive pressures on companies will only increase.

The cloud allows proliferation of best practices at a more rapid pace and a deeper level, enabling managerial innovation and increasing the pace of change. These factors lead to greater "creative destruction" of existing markets and threats to entrenched market leaders. Improved global coordination allows companies that have found unique ways to deliver products in certain markets to go global with those advantages. Traditional business models will feel pressure to improve productivity in order to remain competitive. Market leaders that fail to take advantage of technological innovations will be at risk of forfeiting their lofty status.

Daniel Burton of Salesforce.com said cloud economics, "changes the concept of what is innovation. Suddenly there's this mass innovation system that will be highly disruptive, and it's unclear what the life cycle will be of these new applications that get put out on the cloud. Are they going to have long life cycles? Or are they going to be much shorter because they're going to another entrepreneur who comes along with no overhead, capital or distribution marketing costs and so he can put up something and undercut yours? The whole innovation model is changing, the time to market for new products is picking up speed, and it's all going to have a disruptive effect on businesses and entire industries."

James Manyika of McKinsey & Company held out the success story of ICIC Bank in India, which grew from a market cap of $200 million to $40 billion. He estimated that their IT costs run only perhaps a tenth of a comparable bank in the United States. The environment in which they operate demands lower operating costs, and so they have had to innovate. ICIC has even more challenging requirements when they operate in rural environments and try to offer banking services to the poor. "If they're successful, consider what that would do in a disruptive sense to business models here," Manyika said. "In a similar fashion, think about cell phone operators that have figured out ways to succeed in what are otherwise considered 'hard to serve' environments around the world and the business models they have developed to do that. Think also about the initiatives that some Asian banks are taking with regard to the use of mobile technology for banking. Think about what these models could do if these players and others are able to take these models to other markets: this could be very disruptive. A lot of these models are facilitated by cloud computing, and their potential mobility is also enhanced by the potential reach of cloud computing. What is the disruptive threat? That such innovators could become major players in markets other than in their home countries? That we might see a reverse trend of business models developed in these adverse environments get applied back in developed markets with disruptive effects? I think we will likely see many leading companies both from emerging markets and from developed markets looking to learn from disruptive models developed in the adverse environments and many of them leveraging cloud computing capabilities."

A shift from marketing push to customer pull. The social Web and cloud economy are moving us closer to a product meritocracy, where the superior or greenest product wins, not the one with the best marketing campaign. Since the 1990s the Internet has put power in the hands of individuals to research businesses, products and services, giving rise to consumer and product sites filled with user recommendations (epinions, Amazon, Yelp), user ratings (eBay, Angie's List) and collaborative filtering technologies (Amazon, Netflix, Pandora). With round-the-clock access to information, customers have a new set of expectations about the wide variety of goods and services they want to pull down on demand, and companies have a corresponding set of opportunities to meet them.

On a fundamental level, society is evolving from a push society, where consumer goods are pushed at us by mass marketers, to a pull society, where individuals either proactively search for products and services they need or passively invite businesses to "make me an offer." Internet search makes it easier for buyers to find all the products they should be comparing—not just the ones they have seen advertised on TV. That means that the best product, rather than the best advertising campaign, should determine the sale. Similarly, once a user settles on a product, she can search for online merchants with the best price and a reputable track record (often a customer-generated star rating) worthy of her pocketbook.

Perhaps the most powerful and immediate manifestation of the pull phenomenon will come in the mobile marketplace. Since Apple opened its iPhone to outside developers, millions of people have downloaded thousands of applications to the mobile device, giving them the power to locate nearby taquerias on a street map, play games, share recipes and read books.

At the Web 2.0 Summit in San Francisco in November 2008, a new company called GoodGuide debuted with the ambitious goal of providing "the world's largest and most reliable source of information on the health, environmental and social impacts of the products in your home." Founded by a professor at the University of California at Berkeley, GoodGuide rates a wide range of products across 140 criteria, such as carcinogen levels, carbon footprint and so on. Using your iPhone or mobile device while walking the aisles of your favorite supermarket, you are able to browse the top products in categories such as shampoos or deodorants.

"This will change how millions of Americans shop," O'Rourke told the Web 2.0 Summit attendees. "You'll be able to find safe, healthy and green products, based on the best science in the world, screened for your personal preferences. This will shift the balance of power and ultimately transform the marketplace."[31]

At the roundtable, William Coleman suggested to the participants that "the ultimate evolution of pull is the market of one person." As mass marketing and mass production give way to niche companies making highly differentiated products, "the market of one" will come into being and, over a long period of time, replace the largely undifferentiated mass marketplace that exists today.

> **The social Web and cloud economy are moving us closer to a product meritocracy, where the superior or greenest product wins.**

John Clippinger and John Seely Brown argued that individuals at the edge gain in bargaining power and influence when they form into groups. In some cases these groups will self-organize; in other cases, people will opt into loose-knit aggregated micromarkets that align with their interests or consumer behaviors. The cloud will enhance the credibility and power of these groups or networks partly because the data in the cloud will be controlled—indeed, put there—by individuals and thus will have greater value than information that is extracted or inferred from various databases, Brown said. "That will create a different kind of market. It's not where we are right now."

"Companies are facing a huge mind shift by the public," Esther Dyson said. She welcomes the day when she can alert American Airlines that she is traveling to Los Angeles again next week and she is presented not with a website banner ad but with a specific travel itinerary and fare offer. "I think you're going to see many more vendors becoming part of a community rather than just directing messages at us. They're going to be part of the conversation in a respectful but intimate way. I'm no longer going to be Mrs. Middle-Aged White Lady. I'm going to be Esther Dyson with these specific travel plans, this specific shoe size and a need for a ball gown in October."

Clouds will move from closed to open

Today, Cloud 1.0 is still very much a closed environment, with businesses using cloud architecture as private servers. Over time, as clouds begin to commingle, public or open clouds will enable the cross-pollination of content and services by pulling from different sources and will have an innovation advantage over closed ecosystems.

Several participants, including Esther Dyson and John Seely Brown, saw a need to transition to standards-setting for clouds, with a superstructure that enables interoperability between different parties, datasets and services in a secure way. "I think a key enabler in this is to get the interoperable identity systems right," said John Clippinger, "because then it allows you to do the aggregation, the mash-ups, in the cloud, and that creates the mobility, and I think that creates a different business model."

Ann Winblad, cofounder and managing director of Hummer Winblad Venture Partners, doubted that large institutional players would work in tandem toward facilitating the cloud's widespread adoption because of two factors: the overriding goal of protecting shareholder value tied to existing pricing models and the internal forces in management, such as sales managers, that are wedded to keeping things the way they are. "There are going to be sales people saying, 'What happened to my commission check?' There is going to be resistance from other quarters," she said.

Indeed, that is one of the big question marks hanging over cloud vendors: are there enough customers willing to pay by the drink for this business model to work? While the software-as-a-service model relies on old-fashioned subscriptions, the new utility or grid computing model charges only for what you use. The move from a fixed cost to a variable cost model is still largely unproven.

Corporations that have embraced early versions of the cloud, such as Salesforce or SAP's offering of software as a service, still require considerable upfront fees and will be hesitant to embrace the pay-by-the-drink business model envisioned by the roundtable. "It's a long distance from that model to this more granular metered billing that we've been discussing," Winblad said. She added that "early stage investors like ourselves are going to be very cautious about funding the next generation of application software vendors" if their business models are built on granular "pay by the sip" pricing rather than packaged goods or upfront subscription fees.

Daniel Burton said Salesforce.com is not considering switching to an hourly pricing model. "We're happy with the old-fashioned subscription model. You pay us and we'll let you use our application software on the servers in our data center. By the way, we don't look at the data, we don't know what's in there—whether it's sensitive, strategic, financial or personal."

James Manyika wondered about the business models that will support this expected wave of cloud businesses. People have generally shown an unwillingness to pay for services or products on the Web. Will a micropayments system based on pay-per-use be sufficient to sustain a business? Will these cloud services lure enough users to attract advertisers? "How do you deal with the question of business models in the coming world where we set expectations that most of these things are going to be free?" he asked. There are many valuable services where users have now been conditioned to expect them to be free, such as search, Web mail and others. It appears that many of these services will continue to be free over the long term. The question is, Manyika said, how do these get monetized? "Today's answer is advertising, but it cannot be the only answer for all time. We will likely see many innovators start to tap other profit pools that are adjacent to the free service and activity in the way that advertising is closely associated with search activity."

But online advertising is getting better and smarter all the time, even if those improvements are coming about in small increments. Online retailers have long targeted ads by location, by matching the IP address of users' computers with a physical address. Recently, companies have started customizing the content of their sites based on those locations. They have begun to show swimsuits to people in Florida or parkas in Alaska.[32]

Ann Winblad pointed to the constant experimentation with search and advertising that Varian cited and added: "I might see a different Google than somebody else does when I'm searching. You might also see a different Wal-Mart each time you visit their site because all of these companies already are very skilled at using anonymous data to run multiple versions of their sites to closely target customers—not down to individuals but down to pretty small sets to perfect their anonymous targeting."

John Clippinger said to look for major changes in the way online advertising works in the years ahead, tied to an identity system that has buy-in from both users and businesses. "Advertising today is push. You don't know who your customers are, not really. When you start getting identity systems where people can disclose their preferences and you can aggregate those in the cloud, then the huge cost of markets discovering who your customers are goes away. Couple that with giving users ways of protecting private information and controlling what information they want to disclose with a level of granularity, then I think you're moving to a whole new model. It's going to be more like a reverse auction where you're going to aggregate demand around a limited number of suppliers [in thousands of categories]. You're going to have a learning mechanism and a market that will identify this aggregation of 'spikes,' or suppliers, that meet this very sophisticated demand or pull function on the part of empowered users. Then you'll have this fitness function—a survival of the fittest—that will be working on top of that, driving out the less efficient networks, and all of this is going up the social technology and innovation curve. That's a huge shift. Oh, my God, just look at where advertising on the Internet is heading!"

Cautions about the move to the cloud

As the U.S. economy heads into what may be a prolonged slowdown, and corporate executives show resistance to making expensive long-term capital investments, cloud computing may get a second and third look. "I think the imperative to lower costs in the enterprise is a fundamental trend that is going to have huge impact driving cyber computing forward over the next year," Daniel Burton said.

While lower costs over the long term will spur many executive teams to consider a cloud solution for their IT needs, several roundtable members expressed a note of caution about how quickly corporate America will move into the cloud.

Among the chief issues that may cause companies to proceed with caution:

- *Security.* Is my data safe? Who can access it? Can malware and phishing attacks compromise the data, the applications or the platform in a cloud environment?

- *Reliability.* My business needs to run 24/7 with no downtime—can you guarantee that? What backup systems are in place if a server goes down?

- *Interoperability.* Is my data portable? Does it work across applications or is it cordoned off to a single data silo?

- *Compliance and liability.* Who is at fault if my data is compromised? Where is my data being stored in the cloud? Can I gain access to every facet at all times to comply with Sarbanes-Oxley and other federal laws and regulations? Does the cloud setup meet all risk and compliance mechanisms mandated by regulatory regimes?

A June 2008 white paper by the 451 Group consultancy concluded that cloud computing appears most suited for companies that require only ninety-nine percent uptime, have low bandwidth requirements and do not require especially stringent security.[33]

When large companies weigh the benefits and risks of a move to cloud environments, the issues of security and reliability come to the fore again and again. Some of them have begun to move their least sensitive assets to cloud servers.

"One significant barrier we always underestimate is how much emphasis large enterprises put on the mission-critical nature of their data," said Padmasree Warrior of Cisco Systems. "The cloud model has to address the mission-critical nature of large institutions being always on. Currently it doesn't do that. That doesn't mean it won't evolve to that, but that's a big weakness today in having it deploy widely."

Daniel Burton of Salesforce.com, the enterprise cloud computing company, said the realities of the marketplace will make it unlikely the cloud will bring about a fundamental shift in pricing models for companies offering software as a service applications. "I don't think you're going to see a move to micropayments or hourly payments for software as a service applications any time soon because the security and the reliability requirements are so extreme." Salesforce.com confronted the reliability issue in early 2006 when the company experienced service disruptions that limited customer access to their own data.

Burton said Salesforce.com addressed customer concerns by creating a trust site (*https://trust.salesforce.com*) that shows current system performance and historical system information in a pioneering and transparent way. "Customers can get a real-time view every day of our performance," he said. "You can go in and see what kind of phishing attacks we're seeing, what kind of issues you need to be aware of, and so on. If I'm running my entire business on this cloud platform, I've got to know that it's up and running and have instant access to system performance and security threats."

Implications for Government and Governing

As the Internet evolved over the years, bad actors evolved along with it. In the early days, geeks and hackers broke into networks or released viruses chiefly for kicks, bragging rights or to expose security flaws. A commercial industry was born to prevent malware and spyware from invading users' home computers, and corporate IT departments ramped up their security systems. Despite government's best efforts to criminalize the practice, the onslaught of spam continues unabated to this day.

Next, con artists entered the picture. These "stealth for wealth" scammers flooded us with email ruses (not all of them from Nigerian princes) and phishing, pharming and spoofing schemes to steal one's identifying information or financial passwords. The cat-and-mouse game continues with online identity theft becoming more sophisticated, Web browsers such as Firefox and Internet Explorer implementing phishing warning systems, and users becoming more aware of the threat.

Today, the Internet has become so interwoven into the fabric of our nation's financial system, our business culture and our daily lives that a new worry looms: the threat of a major disruption to the Internet by malicious actors. National security officials have begun to assess the vulnerabilities of Internet protocols and are taking steps to protect potential points of failure. In the commercial sphere, website tracking and targeted advertising are becoming major components of the next-generation Internet, and stakeholders are grappling with issues of digital identity and online privacy.

With so much at stake on the economic and security fronts, government has begun to play a more assertive role in dealing with these issues. Here are several areas that governments are now tackling:

Public policy on identity and privacy. The roundtable members believe policy makers should sort out the myriad interests at stake in the areas of identity, authentication, privacy. Participants recommend convening a White House Summit on Security and Liberty (see Appendix).

Electronic surveillance. Related to this are efforts by governments to identify threats posed by terrorism, organized crime, spammers, child pornography and the like.

Cyber-security. Protection of the nation's IP and telecommunications infrastructure has become a key concern of national security officials. In addition, government agencies have stepped up efforts to protect classified reports and intelligence information in light of efforts by both foreign enemies and allies to gain access to restricted data.

Monitoring and development of the cloud. As market forces propel us toward a "Cloud 3.0" environment for citizens, businesses, organizations, government agencies and other parties, policy makers have a role in monitoring and steering the development of the cloud computing phenomenon so the emerging technological platform meets the needs of all stakeholders. This may include a federal role in technical standard setting for the evolution of the network.

The fact that more and more of our financial, military and governmental institutions are switching over to IP-based systems is both a blessing [and] a huge curse.

Fundamentally, anything that can be attached to the network can be hacked.

On the Russian cyber black market, stolen credit card information sells for $15 per account. A database with 100,000 purloined credit card names and numbers could sell for $1.5 million.

More ominously, the kind of potential for foul play seen in Hollywood thrillers is not too distant from reality. What happens when five kids in Bulgaria break into your defense system and take it down? Or a group of bad actors takes down the entire Internet by breaking DNS [Domain Name System] or BGP [Border Gateway Protocol] so that when you type in 'Google' you get something else?

The transportation company CSX Corp. changed over to an IP-based system for their container-shipping trains not long ago, according to published reports. One can imagine the destruction that could ensue if a terrorist group hacked into its switching system. A host of transportation systems, nuclear power plants and other installations could pose security vulnerabilities unless sufficient safeguards are put into place.

Flash points are already occurring at the nation-state level. In Lebanon a military conflict broke out after the country's Parliament forbade Hezbollah from operating its own Internet network across southern Lebanon for communications, television and ISP service. Hezbollah responded by launching an armed incursion into Beirut, setting up roadblocks and blowing up a key media center. Some 40 people were killed. The government was forced to reverse itself and cede control of the Internet network in southern Lebanon to Hezbollah.

Today, it is not who controls the printing press that matters—it is who controls the network. Tomorrow, it may be about who controls the cloud.

Security, privacy and civil liberties

During the September 11 terrorist attacks, one of the few communications systems that proved resilient was phone-to-phone texting. Those snippets of text traveled twice as far, but more reliably, than calls directed to the cell towers atop the Twin Towers. The digital messages do not hop onto the Internet unless the parties use different carriers. Today, government officials are trying to map out how to create a redundant or replacement network that would keep SMS [short message service] working should the Internet fail. Similar efforts are being made to re-architect the emergency broadcast system.

The Internet cannot be made completely impervious to attack, but that vulnerability is also a strength. "The very thing that makes a network maximally resilient under random failure is exactly what makes it maximally open to terrorist attack," said John Seely Brown, independent co-chair at the Deloitte Center for Edge Innovation. "The Internet was designed to be this maximally resilient system, and that's why it would be easy for a terrorist to take the entire network down—because scale-free networks are maximally open to attack."

In April 2008, *Business Week* magazine reported on the rising attacks on America's most sensitive computer networks and the "startling" security gaps it uncovered:

> The U.S. government, and its sprawl of defense con-
> tractors, have been the victims of an unprecedented
> rash of similar cyber attacks over the last two years, say
> current and former U.S. government officials. "It's
> espionage on a massive scale," says Paul B. Kurtz, a for-
> mer high-ranking national security official.
> Government agencies reported 12,986 cyber security
> incidents to the U.S. Homeland Security Department
> last fiscal year, triple the number from two years earli-
> er. Incursions on the military's networks were up 55%
> last year, says Lieutenant General Charles E. Croom,
> head of the Pentagon's Joint Task Force for Global
> Network Operations. Private targets like Booz Allen are
> just as vulnerable and pose just as much potential secu-
> rity risk. 'They have our information on their net-
> works. They're building our weapon systems. You
> wouldn't want that in enemy hands,' Croom says.
> Cyber attackers 'are not denying, disrupting, or
> destroying operations—yet. But that doesn't mean they
> don't have the capability.'[34]

More than 20 countries now have the ability to commit acts of cyber warfare or cyber aggression. It is becoming more difficult to tell the difference between foreign powers' actions that probe U.S. intelligence capabilities, efforts to penetrate our system to obtain classified information and botnet attacks that jam or bring down systems. "One of the challenges in the online world is that the boundaries between intelligence gathering, cyberwarfare and crime are so blurred," Symantec's Mark Bregman said.

While foreign governments, including even some allies, probe the capabilities of U.S. intelligence systems—and, no doubt, the opposite is true as well—Paul Romer of Stanford observed that global economic interdependence makes it unlikely a nation-state would attempt to bring down Wall Street or the banking system. "Cloud computing actually can become a catalyst to create such complex economic interdependency that you almost can't launch a cyber attack because you risk damaging yourself as much as you damage your target," he said.

Such norms apply only to rational actors and not to terrorists and bad actors bent on inflicting as much destruction as possible. Just as companies are now being "born global," so too are terrorist and radical organizations who no longer are encumbered by issues of scale or national boundaries. The good news, if still only a glimmer, is that as economic, financial and political institutions become more interconnected, accessible and dependent on the Internet, all governments may have a vested interest in cracking down on malevolent forces within their borders.

It is also out of business self-interest and a recognition of the interconnected global economy that many large companies such as Cisco Sytems do participate with the U.S. Department of Defense and other agencies in simulation exercises to advance national security objectives, said Cisco Systems CTO Padmasree Warrior.

Several executives of major corporations in the room pointed to a little-discussed phenomenon: the hesitance of multinational corporations to store data on servers that sit on United States soil. A perception exists in the commercial world that the U.S. government—through the National Security Agency, CIA, Justice Department, FBI and its counterparts among U.S. allies—can gain access to sensitive corporate data through use of the Patriot Act. As a result, more and more large companies are storing their sensitive data in secure locations overseas.

"The cloud is a huge problem to the business model of these companies," Salesforce's Daniel Burton said, because as the data becomes balkanized, the company no longer knows where the data resides—and under which government's jurisdiction it may be subject to subpoena.

Max Mancini of eBay was among those who pointed to the erosion of trust, both at home and abroad, in our ability to protect information because of national security concerns. "If we don't fix that, developing countries that don't have the same barriers and offer comparable technology and infrastructure will pass us by economically very quickly. China won't because they have the same trust problem, but other countries certainly have that potential, and I think that can do a significant amount of damage to our ability to lead on the technology and economic fronts."

Several roundtable participants pointed out the inherent tension between privacy and civil rights versus government's legitimate interests in maintaining order and security.

Living in the cloud does not put one beyond the government's reach. For example, as Marc Rotenberg of EPIC noted, email sent through Google's service (Gmail) is encrypted from the user to the host (Google) and from the host to the recipient, but the government, with the proper subpoenas, could demand that Google turn over email records between the two parties.

The roundtable members concurred that governments will play a more forceful role in setting technical standards for the future development of the Internet. "We have to establish much stronger cooperation between industry and government and among governments, because every issue today has global dimensions to it," Lucio Stanca of Rome told the group.

At the same time, roundtable participants called for caution in the event that governments overreach and try to impose restrictions on the free flow of information. Some IT managers have warned about laws that require companies to store their data within various nations' borders, requiring cloud providers to build more data centers than are needed just to comply with many different regulatory regimes. Some industry leaders have floated the idea of "free-trade zones" for data centers, where common rules would apply.

Some observers fear that, with personal information spread everywhere and nowhere, the cloud will fall under local jurisdictions to be adjudicated under local privacy, obscenity, hate crime and libel laws, just as Yahoo! and other search engines have been hauled into court in Germany, France and elsewhere. As one participant put it, "The cloud may be global, but the climate will sometimes be local."

Striking the right balance

Lucio Stanca said the issue was not one of control or jurisdiction but rather how to strike the right balance between personal privacy and the need to protect the citizenry from harm. He suggested that there need to be national or international bodies charged with the mandate to "resolve the conflicting needs of security and privacy."

He pointed out that many countries in Europe have already adopted standards for digital signatures to facilitate online transactions; such coordinated efforts lag in the United States.

In addition, participants made note of the changing dynamic between government and citizenry, with users now empowered to organize themselves, interact with elected officials and demand accountability from government agencies and private industry. "It's a new world, and this has very profound implications for democracy," Stanca said.

While the rise of the empowered user offers great social benefit for participation, civic engagement and collaboration, it also empowers those with darker motivations. "It's very clear that the downside of technological change is that it gives individuals the power to do great harm," Paul Romer said. From the Unabomber to the anthrax attacks to Al Qaeda, individuals now have the ability to disrupt our lives and impose tragic consequences on a scale few imagined only a few years ago.

The result, Romer suggested, is that such acts of mayhem "will inevitably push us further in the direction of preemption, prevention and surveillance." As the damage any individual can do goes up, we will inevitably adjust the tradeoff between liberty and security.

An incident that occurred in San Francisco in July 2008 demonstrated the power that knowledgeable specialists now wield over large institutions and the public. San Francisco IT administrator Terry Childs was arrested and charged with four counts of computer tampering after he refused to give over passwords to the Cisco Systems switches and routers used on the city's FiberWAN network, which carries about 60 percent of the municipal government's network traffic. He agreed to hand over the passwords only after meeting personally with San Francisco Mayor Gavin Newsom.[35]

The threats we face in the future will increasingly come not from nation-states but from individuals, rogue terrorist cells and hard-to-anticipate sources that launch spontaneous attacks through unconventional methods.

"How do you deal with those threats?" asked Kim Taipale, founder of the Center for Advanced Studies in Science and Technology. "I believe that the security conversation, the identity conversation and the privacy conversation are the same conversation." National security is becoming dependent on the ability of intelligence agents to discern credible threats posed by individuals and small groups, not just other nation-states.

Even on a nation-state level, the Cold War has given way to a new paradigm of simultaneous cooperation and conflict between nations. Taipale said China and the United States are unlikely to engage in a protracted shooting war, and yet the two nations "are going to be in constant conflict, cooperation and competition at the same time."

Taipale called for adopting a new breed of security model that consists of multiple layers. "We don't get rid of the old model, but there's a new layer that's on top that is based on the public health model, which is based on global cooperation, based on a combination of syndromic surveillance, early identification of potential threats, isolation of the problem, trying to prevent an epidemic but understanding that there are going to be pathogens loose in the system—and that those pathogens are going to be inside the system, not on the outside."

> **Society will have to decide what government's role is, how much responsibility people will take on themselves and what kind of risk management to accept on a societal level.**
>
> *Kim Taipale*

Society will have to decide what government's role is, how much responsibility people will take on themselves and what kind of risk management to accept on a societal level, Taipale said. "Do we really look only to government to make us safe or do we take on some communal responsibility? I think in this context the private sector has to take on communal responsibility. The answer cannot be to relegate all aspects of security to the government's national security apparatus. Today national security is really global security, and the only way we can achieve a measure of real global security is to open up our systems and cooperate with our competitors—whether corporations or other nation-states—on security."

Implications for Personal Well-being

The great potential of the new information and communications technologies is to make everyone's lives easier, more efficient, longer lasting and more pleasant in performing tasks that we enjoy. The rise of the social Web and the follow-on movement toward a Web presence in the cloud presents extraordinary opportunities for advancing personal well-being. At the same time, these emerging megatrends are fraught with peril: to privacy, liberty and identity.

The cloud's impact on our everyday lives has obvious and not-so-obvious benefits.

Productivity has increased in recent years partly because of the cloud. The explosion in Web-based email services starting in the 1990s—Hotmail, Yahoo! Mail and now Google's Gmail—freed users from the tyranny of the desktop. In 2008, these services serve 256 million, 255 million and 92 million registered users, respectively.[36] The idea that a businesswoman or user has to sit down at a particular machine to check one's email is rapidly becoming an antiquated concept. Now it is possible to stay in constant contact with peers—through email, SMS and (at times) chat—on BlackBerry, iPhone, cell phone, netbook or mobile laptop.

Web 2.0 applications have advanced to the point where large companies and small startups often find that Web-based applications—Google Docs, 37signals' Basecamp, collaborative tools from Salesforce.com, Zoho and other vendors—provide greater efficiency than passing spreadsheets and Word documents back and forth.

A long-term cultural shift is taking place in the dynamics of organized work. Corporations in the 20th century were organized under a command-and-control system for organizing interactions among large numbers of people. Businesses in the new century are moving in a different direction: away from centralized, top-down control and toward more distributed, peer-oriented organizational structures. In fact, many companies are virtual global firms with multiple employees and no central offices. The long-held fantasy about working on a tropical beach is becoming a reality for many entrepreneurs, in part thanks to the cloud.

Weighing risks vs. benefits

How can individuals maintain control over their own identity and personal information in this new world? Where is the line between protection of individuals against terrorists and criminals, and personal liberties? What are the potential unintended consequences to the individual and to society?

Three areas that deserve special attention are electronic health records, crime prevention and detection, and social networks.

The past year has seen dramatic advances in the development of models for online access to medical information, EPIC's Marc Rotenberg told the roundtable. Major players vying for a slice of the marketplace include Google Health, Microsoft's Health Vault, and Dossia—an independent nonprofit infrastructure created by a consortium of large employers for gathering and storing information for life-long health records.

"There could be enormous benefits in the delivery of healthcare service in the United States, reduction of costs and improvements in research, but it's also reasonable to suggest that there might be enormous risks involved," Rotenberg said. "Certainly we know that medical information is the most sensitive information and has enormous impact in the workforce in terms of employment decisions. There are some very interesting questions about the use of genetic markers when it comes to employment practices. Congress tried to address that recently by passing the Genetic Information Non-Discrimination Act. So we need to ask a few questions with some of these models: who collects the data, how is the data used, who has access to the data, what are the risks of collecting and sharing the data? One interesting question in the context of cloud computing might turn out to be who is responsible when there is a problem. Who is the custodian of the record, and what happens if there's a significant data breach or misuse? When sensitive information like medical records move into the cloud, these questions become particularly important."

Crime detection and prevention take on almost Orwellian overtones as identifying information about criminals and citizens becomes easier to share—and perhaps more difficult to correct, amend or delete. Rotenberg showed stills of scenes of Tom Cruise in *Minority Report* and Ethan Hawke in *Gattaca* as cautionary tales about giving the government too much power to thwart crime—before it even happens—and authenticate identity.

Only science fiction, right? But Rotenberg reminded the group that a Bush administration proposal for Total Information Awareness came to light in 2002:

> In November 2002, *The New York Times* reported that the Defense Advanced Research Projects Agency (DARPA) was developing a tracking system called

"Total Information Awareness" (TIA), which was intended to detect terrorists through analyzing troves of information. The system, developed under the direction of John Poindexter, then-director of DARPA's Information Awareness Office, was envisioned to give law enforcement access to private data without suspicion of wrongdoing or a warrant.

TIA purported to capture the "information signature" of people so that the government could track potential terrorists and criminals involved in "low-intensity/low-density" forms of warfare and crime. The goal was to track individuals through collecting as much information about them as possible and using computer algorithms and human analysis to detect potential activity.

The project called for the development of "revolutionary technology for ultra-large all-source information repositories," which would contain information from multiple sources to create a "virtual, centralized, grand database." This database would be populated by transaction data contained in current databases such as financial records, medical records, communication records, and travel records as well as new sources of information. Also fed into the database would be intelligence data.

A key component of the TIA project was to develop data-mining or knowledge discovery tools that would sort through the massive amounts of information to find patterns and associations. TIA would also develop search tools such as Project Genoa, which Admiral Poindexter's former employer Syntek Technologies assisted in developing. TIA aimed to fund the development of more such tools and data-mining technology to help analysts understand and even "preempt" future action.

A further crucial component was the development of biometric technology to enable the identification and tracking of individuals. DARPA had already funded its "Human ID at a Distance" program, which aimed to positively identify people from a distance through technologies such as face recognition or gait recognition.[37]

The heart of the data-mining proposal—to collect, synthesize and share large amounts of information about individuals, collected from disparate agencies, in a central government database—raised such a public outcry that Congress shuttered the program in 2003.

A number of state governments are considering establishing new data sharing centers called fusion centers that combine information from federal, state and local law enforcement intelligence databases, Rotenberg pointed out. "The big question, I think, is should there be any legal limits to the types of information that should be available to government?"

In addition, both the U.S. government and the private sector continue to develop new surveillance techniques based on such biometrics identifiers as facial topology or the gait of one's walk. In the United Kingdom, the widespread use of camera surveillance is evolving into new techniques for tracking, such as city-wide license plate readers as well as criminal fines for people who try to defeat these systems. The Chinese government has led the world in developing and deploying biometric identification systems. It has installed in public places 20,000 facial recognition cameras, built by Connecticut-based L-1 Identity Solutions.

Finally, 2009 will bring about the ultimate in transparency: the rollout of total body imaging devices at U.S. airports to identify risks to aviation security that cannot be detected by traditional magnetometers.

Social networks will continue their mesmerizing hold on the public's attention, Rotenberg said, and "individuals will gain a better understanding of the consequences of distributing personal information across multiple platforms." The possible pitfalls of letting companies use one's personal data for their own benefit burst into the public consciousness in November 2007, when Facebook's "Beacon" system of publicizing online purchases to one's friends without consent became a public relations disaster.

As with email and websites, Rotenberg said, there are profound privacy issues that need to be addressed with social networks. "The goal should be to construct a policy framework that provides guidance and direction for new laws, techniques and practices that will encourage the benefits of social network services and minimize the risks," he said.

Personalization: Context is everything

The roundtable took up the issue of the increasing granularity in the transaction space, where the overarching trend is from mass marketing to tiny niche markets—ultimately a marketplace of one—and where the emphasis would be on finely tuned algorithms or bots pulling buying opportunities out of the cloud rather than having advertisers and marketers pushing their wares. The first generation of these pull services is already here in the form of email alerts, RSS feeds and SMS messages that match criteria—for instance, a used British roadster in the color red—set by the user.

Today the holy grail of marketing has turned to targeted advertising, where two consumers viewing the same website would receive different marketing messages based on their browsing history, purchasing history or other criteria. To the extent that users do not opt into such arrangements, this is still very much a push world, with marketers operating under the premise that consumers do not always know what they want or need. But society is evolving toward pull models on multiple levels.

"Corporations can no longer push products on people," said Kim Taipale of the Center for Advanced Studies in Science and Technology. "They need to pull consumers in. In much the same way, the U.S. government will have to conduct policy on a pull basis rather than a push basis by exercising soft power instead of hard power."

At the user and consumer level, Taipale said, the bottom-line question comes down to, "Is personalization something that is done to you or done for you?" He suggested the answer changes in different circumstances, and the benefits and drawbacks of the arrangement between buyer, seller and transaction agent vary from situation to situation.

The locus of control and permissions should begin with the individual—the model of "user-centricity," Taipale said. The roundtable participants concurred. When corporations make decisions about selling or giving access to individuals' data, society must decide the appropriate boundaries and enact laws where necessary. Defaults matter, and the technology systems and legal devices society constructs affect the balance of power between individuals and institutions. The choice between opt-out and opt-in becomes not just a technical choice but a significant policy question.

Facebook has become a key player in the public's growing expectation that individuals should be able to control their own personal data, said Esther Dyson. "The goal, I think, should be to give the individual both maximum knowledge and control over their data." The site may even be nudging users into becoming more proactive in exercising those controls. (Daniel Burton pointed out the irony that Facebook is not a cloud computing company, given that it does not offer servers to outside developers, but it has been the key company helping define the contours of the social Web.)

Outside the United States, social networks like Bebo and hi5 in Europe and CyWorld in South Korea tend to be based more on financial transactions than the social transactions of Facebook, observed Anna Lysyanskaya. At many of these sites, the focus is on the sale of music or virtual goods, and so the interactions fall more in line with expectations about the exchange of money for commercial wares.

In the future, Dyson said, there will be even more granularity around permitted access to your own genetic information. Already the genetic testing service 23andme.com lets you discover how your genes influence your health and traits by genotyping your DNA for $399. "Knowing more about our own genetic makeup allows us to make better decisions about our lives and our health. That in turn will lead to a raft of new companies and products that will provide us with better information and recommendations tailored to our unique genetic makeup and physical characteristics, along with a lot of tailored spam!" Dyson said. That additional genetic data "can be a burden as well as an advantage, because knowledge often requires people to make more decisions or manage their behavior, and feel responsible for the consequences. Accidents happen, but if you 'knew' you were vulnerable to X, then perhaps it's your fault if you did not take the proper precautions. How much sympathy does [New Jersey governor] Jon Corzine, who was not wearing his seat belt in a car crash, deserve? How much does a smoker who gets lung cancer? And in the future, what will we expect of people whose genes make them susceptible to something they might be able to avoid by a behavior change? Like any other kind of information, genetic information can be extremely disruptive."

Geographic and cultural factors also play a role in properly weighting the scales of privacy. "If I'm in France or Germany and all my health care is being paid for or delivered by a society-supported system, the power equation around access to electronic health and medical records is a little different than what it is in the United States, where there's a more market-based system," said Harriet Pearson, chief privacy officer of IBM. But regardless of region, the key to balancing individual privacy and modern uses of health information is good public policy, good education and strong information governance within those institutions that steward such sensitive data. Kim Taipale added that in Europe the emphasis in conversations about privacy of personal data is on restraining the behavior of corporations, not governments.

But in every country, the participants concurred, we need to begin thinking about giving people the ability to exert a measure of control over—and understanding of—their data, whether in private or government hands. "We're facing a new kind of digital divide in terms of people's ability to understand the implications of what their private data means, how it's shared in the cloud, and so on," Mark Bregman said. "We sit here talking about our DNA markers, and a large part of the world's population can't spell DNA, and yet it holds great significance for us all."

The digital divide is devolving into a participation divide, John Seely Brown suggested. "This is not something you learn about. This is something you become, and you won't necessarily understand the implications unless you are an active participant in the online world."

John Clippinger agreed and suggested that user-centricity falls short if people are forced to make a lot of complex decisions. Instead, what naturally happens is a proxy or surrogate whom people trust acts on their behalf. For example, a consumer or advocacy group or doctors' group could develop a set of best practices around the disclosure of medical information. The idea of creating an easy-to-use set of tools that give individuals the ability to fine-tune who should have access to certain sets of personal data may seem formidable but, as Anna Lysyanskaya argued, "We already have the technology that allows you do to this kind of thing. Perhaps we should be thinking about how to develop the technology and the educational programs, how to create business models to solve the problems and deliver the benefits so we get to a win-win solution."

Users may take the easiest, most convenient route, regardless of what may be in their best interests. One participant pointed to the effort a decade ago to promote trust and confidence in new e-commerce sites through the Platform for Privacy Preferences (P3P), which Microsoft implemented as an option in Internet Explorer 6. Yet only a tiny fraction of users changed the browser's default setting to take advantage of the ability to let users decide how much personal data they want to reveal to a website.

> **The digital divide is devolving into a participation divide.**
>
> *John Seely Brown*

Normally consumers will take the path of least resistance, whether they are interacting with the government or with corporations. At the same time, as one participant pointed out, most corporations take the view that the more user data they acquire the more they will be able to extract value and maximize profit for shareholders.

The evidence so far suggests that marketers have the upper hand in coaxing personal information such as buying preferences or demographic data out of users for incentives that amount to a pittance. The website *Socialmedia.com* creates Facebook widgets such as Food Fight or Happy Hour that contain market research surveys. The company works with clients to collect user profile data such as ages, political views, mortgage status, favorite candy and so on. It receives more than a million responses a day. How does the company cajole these personal tidbits out of Facebook members? By offering "points" that let them buy more virtual food to throw at their friends or buy their friends another virtual drink.[38]

One participant cited the example of the British headquarters of Safeway. "I once had an interesting meeting with a data guy there who showed me some data they gathered about their consumers. I said, 'Wow this is really detailed. How did you get this?' and he said, 'We offered them a coupon for a doughnut and a cup of coffee.' People will give away private information for almost any compensation."

Perhaps the biggest shift in the privacy and identity arena has been a cultural one, at least in the United States. With the exponential growth of photo-sharing sites, video-sharing sites and social networking sites since 2005, the zone of privacy has shrunken significantly as the digital generation embraces media sharing and transparency and worries less about traditional privacy concerns.

Aedhmar Hynes pointed out that the same culture of transparency has not taken hold in other societies, such as Japan, where people are more "comfortable culturally" with remaining anonymous online. On Mixi, the largest social network in Japan, fewer than five percent of its fifteen million members use real names or photos.[39]

In the United States, as abuses of people's personal data grow—whether from corporations performing data-mining or phishing scams that unlock online accounts—the public may begin to grow more protective and discerning about security and personal identity.

While consumers are swimming in a sea of information, they do not have powerful constituent-based organizations advocating to redress the balance of power between individuals and institutions that are building power based on these warehouses of data. The groups that do advocate effectively for the public, such as the Electronic Privacy Information Center and the Center for Democracy & Technology, are massively outgunned and do not have a broad base of constituents, participants noted.

Michael DeNoma of Standard Chartered, PLC observed that there are few constraints on companies holding quite sensitive information about individuals. Even in the banking and financial services sector, which historically have been more heavily regulated, the penalties associated with mishandling sensitive, personal information today are moderate to low.

While cloud computing companies are not heavily regulated, Salesforce.com's Daniel Burton pointed out, "they're hypersensitive about handling data. There is huge reputation risk to their brand and business model" if they misuse data from individuals or businesses.

Conclusion: Market Forces Meet Public Policy

The real impact of cloud computing may be this: in the future, everyone becomes an entrepreneur. In a 2008 report, Bernstein analyst Jeffrey Lindsay wrote:

> No government initiative or five-year strategic plan could have hoped to have achieved anything so profound—Google and Amazon are literally pushing the frontiers of global capitalism right down to the teenager's bedroom. Forget cutting lawns or waiting tables to earn some money, the next generation of college kids are more likely to pay for tuition by showing the world how to play the riff in Weezer's Sweater song by Rivers Cuomo.[40]

Lauren Luke, who lives in Tynesdie, UK, has found her niche in the cloud. Her business model? She applies makeup, videotapes the process, uploads the tutorial to YouTube and gets an ad split from Google. Thousands of other global entrepreneurs are running similar microbusinesses. If the roundtable participants are right, that number will grow to hundreds of millions in the decades ahead as the cloud becomes ubiquitous.

> "The cloud represents the reinvention of commerce...the control point has shifted so that suddenly commerce and communication are end to end, with no regard to borders."
>
> *William Coleman*

The cloud is also liberating us from our desktops and laptops. A new generation of smart phones and broadband-enabled portable devices—including small, low-power netbooks and mids (mobile internet devices)—allow us to wirelessly jack into the cloud continuously to access our personal lifestreams. The amount of digital information in the world will double in the next 18 months, and society will lean increasingly on cloud services to help contextualize its fast-moving personal, business or entertainment experiences—and make sense of the world.

William Coleman, whose writings led to the convening of this roundtable, assayed the landscape this way: "The cloud represents the reinvention of commerce, from a push to pull model and from mass to micromarket economics as the Long Tail dominates value creation enabled by network effects, which accelerates globalization, greatly increases productivity and improves the quality of life for all. The control point has shifted so that suddenly commerce and communication are end to end—with no regard to borders—location and even time independent. We are just at the beginning of an escalating slope of change that affects how we will live socially, culturally, politically. This is a once-in-a-millennium paradigm shift."

Mark Bregman said the forces of globalization, which the cloud will only help accelerate, are one of the most striking aspects of where this is all heading. "When I think about my father's generation, he was concerned with improving the quality of life for him and his kids as Americans, and maybe there was a small degree of interest in helping to lift up Europe because of cultural affinities. But my daughter's generation has a global outlook. She sees herself as a citizen of the world. She has friends all over the globe. She's connected at some level with what happens in China, India, Saudi Arabia or Vietnam."

That global marketplace for goods, services, information and ideas will only grow more pervasive as digital natives turn us into an always-connected culture. The iPhone and other smart phones are quickly changing the mobile landscape. At the Apple App Store, where people downloaded more than 100 million applications in its first two months, many of the programs connect to the cloud, including news feeds, multiplayer games and services that walk you to the nearest sushi bar. Couple those trends in GPS and mobile technology with the prospect of a billion new identity-enabled cell phones, and traditional hierarchies will crumble as power flows from institutions to individuals.

Memo to the new president

At the time of the roundtable, it was unclear who would be taking office in January 2009, but the participants offered a list of policy proposals as well as general advice for the incoming administration.

Said Max Mancini, "I would tell the new president we're on the cusp of significant acceleration and technical capabilities that will drive economic growth, new business opportunities and accelerated innovation, but significant barriers exist. Solving the identity issue is a key to enabling this technical capability. Over the past several years trust has seriously eroded, and that trust must be rebuilt through action by government, private industry and individuals. We must create new partnerships with the private sector in a transparent way to drive an agenda of innovation and progress."

Jeffrey Dachis proposed that a main role of government is to identify and neutralize bad actors and rogue entities, and then to let the distributed computing produce an emergent outcome, one that we cannot predict. "What we can really do is affect the structure of our institutions, the structure of our learning, the structure of our organizations, the structure of our government to embrace and support this emerging cloud of activity."

At the roundtable's conclusion, the participants offered advice for the incoming administration in several areas around information technology policy:

Policy proposals

- *Formulate an identity agenda.* Marc Rotenberg cited Federal Trade Commission [FTC] statistics showing 258,427 cases of identity theft reported to the FTC in 2007. Consumers reported total losses from fraud of more than $1.2 billion.[41] The government should abandon efforts to create a national identity card and instead formulate an agenda that affirms privacy and identity rights, beginning with throwing its weight behind efforts to create a set of open identity standards that individuals, the private sector and other stakeholders will develop. Harriet Pearson said a forward-looking set of policies on security, privacy and identity management would go a long way to building trust in government's ability to manage identity information. Esther Dyson proposed tying persistent identity to actionable information as a way to incentivize positive behaviors and reduce health care costs.

- *Mend the Patriot Act.* Several roundtable members pointed to the data drain taking place, with major corporations refusing to store sensitive information on servers based in the United States and financial institutions moving funds offshore because of the lack of trust engendered by government implementation of the Patriot Act. In addition, security risks need to be weighed against loss of civil liberties, loss of intellectual capital, loss of tourism income and so on. Cyber security is a particular area that needs reexamination.

- *Retraining and immigration reform.* Roundtable participants called on the government to institute a national retraining effort to modernize the U.S. workforce for the new economy. Coupled with this, members called on Congress to enact immigration policies that permit more highly skilled temporary workers entry into the country so the U. S. retains its competitive edge in the technology industry.

- *Modernize the grid.* As part of the administration's energy policy, it should upgrade the national energy grid in an effort to revitalize our core infrastructure enablers. Arjun Gupta harked back to the transcontinental railroad and national highway program as precedents for a bold effort to upgrade the nation's power supply and curtail carbon emissions while laying the foundation for the economic opportunities of the cloud. "This is the biggest single thing the president could do to restore U.S. competitiveness," he said.

- *Deploy world-class broadband.* Arturo Artom called on the government to work with the private sector to build out a high-speed broadband network in all sections of the country to keep America competitive in the cloud economy. He noted that people in European countries get 10 times the speed at less than half the price, and South Korea and Japan are even further ahead.

- *Support an open cloud.* Traditional notions that governments should hoard data within their borders is an outdated notion with the advent of the global cloud economy. We need to pursue architectures that allow individuals, companies and governments to plug into the best resources on the planet, regardless of where they are located. Summoning Padmasree Warrior's vision of interconnected open clouds, the private sector needs to architect the clouds to be able to drift and have the data where it needs to be.

Governing process

- *Restore trust.* A top priority of the new administration is to repair the American public's erosion of trust in the integrity of government institutions and restore the world's trust in U.S. foreign policy as a force for good.

- *Use soft power, not hard power.* Global opinion matters. When influencing foreign public opinion and foreign governments, the United States has proven much more effective in advancing a democratic agenda and fostering goodwill when using soft power rather than invoking a rigid, uncompromising foreign policy. Daniel Burton said, "There is a strategic importance in understanding the world of global cloud platforms, and on a broader level you've got to elevate the importance of soft power, because you're not going to win in the twenty-first century just by using hard power." Aedhmar Hynes suggested that federal officials need to step outside of a U.S.-centric policymaking silo to understand how other nations "perceive brand America."

- *Embrace technological change.* A common theme running through participants' recommendations was that traditional hierarchies and social structures will be supplanted by open systems that are highly networked, borderless, transparent, decentralized and participative. While this process of creative destruction will create disruptions in markets and industries, existing stakeholders should not be propped up by the government. "The new president should be aware of the transformative nature of this new technology," Mark Bregman said. "Cloud computing, identity and privacy are enablers and cornerstones of this new reality."

- *Government partnership, not control.* "The government will have to recognize that they're going to be one of many players with divergent interests in this space, along with the private sector, NGOs and other parties, and they're not going to dictate events like they could in the old world," Kim Taipale said. J.D. Lasica cited Barack Obama's call for bottom-up change that can manifest itself not through agency directives but from public-private partnerships, collaborative efforts and ad hoc social networks.

- *Foster innovation.* The government should encourage a culture of innovation—including the recognition that experimentation and failure need to be embraced—at all levels of government and industry, and it should deliver targeted government services in the cloud in ways that protect privacy interests. A good start would be to internally adopt appropriate Web 2.0 and cloud tools and technologies to promote productivity within federal agencies. John Clippinger said the area of authenticated anonymity is ripe for experimentation.

• *Grow government transparency.* By shining a light into decision-making processes that shape public policy, we will be able to go back and fix things to bring about better outcomes. Esther Dyson added that transparency is only the first step—public information also needs to be intelligible and accessible by the citizenry.

• *Regulate smartly.* The federal government has an interest in such areas as privacy rights, national security (see Appendix for the White House Summit on Security and Liberty proposal), growing the economy and looking after the health and well-being of its citizens. Many of the trends in communications technology outlined in this report bear watching, but there is no way to tell what the rules should look like three to five years from now. As standards and policies evolve for the world of cloud economics, the government should tread lightly and recall the admonition "First, do no harm."

Education

• *Education and research.* Anna Lysyanskaya cited the need to educate citizens about how they can take charge of their data and identity in the emerging cloud. She also called for programs to strengthen math education and reinvigorate the scientific research community as ways to keep our society competitive. John Seely Brown proposed to radically transform No Child Left Behind or replace it with programs to get students engaged in building things that involve science and technology, possibly starting with a national competition.

• *Literacy programs.* J.D. Lasica called for a national endowment to promote media and news literacy and educational programs focusing on identity, privacy and security in the context of the enormous changes taking place in the media industry and social media networks. Charlie Firestone added the need for literacy around the responsibilities of citizenship and the impact of cloud computing technologies on society.

In closing

William Coleman offered this bit of advice: "My message to the next president is: During your possible two terms in office we're going to see potentially the underpinnings of the greatest change in society and economy in over a century. Please understand the significance of that."

The cloud will usher in a seismic shift in the locus of control in our culture, and it will have ripple effects in all walks of life—energy, the environment, national security, learning, health care, business processes, emerging markets and much more. The cloud is about open access, rapid delivery of services, the ability to scale quickly and the power of networks. Ultimately, though, the cloud story is not just about computing, communication or information but about empowering citizens.

Charlie Firestone, executive director of the Aspen Institute Communications and Society Program, closed the roundtable with these words: "In the end, we're going to need the human element. Technology won't be enough. We're going to need the knowledge and wisdom and participation and the will that only people can provide."

Notes

1. Celia Hannon, "The Video Republic," opendemocracy.net, Oct. 6, 2008. Online at: http://www.opendemocracy.net/blog/yes/celia-hannon/2008/10/06/the-video-republic

2. "Going Into Battle," *Newsweek*, p. 75, Nov. 17, 2008.

3. Andrea James: "Hello Animoto, an Amazon Web Services darling," Seattle Post-Intelligencer blog, July 8, 2008. Online at: http://blog.seattlepi.nwsource.com/amazon/archives/142569.asp

4. "Use of Cloud Computing Applications and Services," Internet & American Life Project, September 2008. PDF online at: http://www.pewinternet.org/pdfs/PIP_Cloud.Memo.pdf

5. Irving Wladawsky Berger: "Cloud Computing Promise and Reality," AlwaysOn blog, July 14, 2008. Online at: http://alwayson.goingon.com/permalink/post/28058

6. James Staten: "Is Cloud Computing Ready For The Enterprise?," Forrester Research, March 7, 2008. Online behind a pay firewall at: http://www.forrester.com/Research/Document/Excerpt/0,7211,44229,00.html

7. Daryl C. Plummer, et al: "Cloud Computing: Defining and Describing an Emerging Phenomenon," Gartner, June 17, 2008. Online at: http://www.star.net.uk/resources/star/home/misc/email_images/gartner%20cloud_computing_defining_and_156220.pdf

8. Spencer Reiss: "Cloud Computing, Available at Amazon.com Today," *Wired* magazine, April 21, 2008. Online at: http://www.wired.com/techbiz/it/magazine/16-05/mf_amazon

9. SAP White Paper, "Toward a European Strategy for the Future Internet: A Call for Action," September 2008. PDF online at: http://www.europeansoftware.org/documents/SAP_WP_FutureInternet.pdf

10. "What the Hell is Cloud Computing?," AlwaysOn Network, Aug. 3, 2008. Online at: http://alwayson.goingon.com/permalink/post/28384

11. Galen Gruman: "Early experiments in cloud computing," InfoWord, April 7, 2008. Online at: http://www.infoworld.com/article/08/04/07/15FE-cloud-computing-utility_1.html

12. Galen Gruman

13. Galen Gruman

14. "The long nimbus," *The Economist*, Oct. 23, 2008. Online at: http://www.economist.com/specialreports/displaystory.cfm?story_id=12411864

15. "Where the cloud meets the ground," *The Economist*, Oct. 23, 2008. Online at: http://www.economist.com/specialreports/displaystory.cfm?story_id=12411920

James Manyika noted that cloud data centers make up eighteen percent (and growing) of all data centers, while data centers that serve only an enterprise's internal needs still make up eighty-two percent of the marketplace.

16. David Bollier: "The Rise of Collective Intelligence", The Aspen Institute Communications & Society Program, 2007. Online at: http://staging.aspeninstitute.org/sites/default/files/content/docs/communications%20and%20society%20program/C&S2007INFOTECHREPORT.PDF

17. For a fuller discussion of digital identity, the annual Digital ID World conference is a rich source of information. Details at: conference.digitalidworld.com/

18. Doc Searls: "The Intention Economy," Linux Journal, March 8, 2006. Online at: http://www.linuxjournal.com/node/1000035

19. Windows Family of Products: "Windows CardSpace helps you control your digital identity and use the Internet more securely." Online at: http://www.microsoft.com/windows/products/winfamily/cardspace/default.mspx

20. For more information about i-cards, see Wikipedia: i-card at http://en.wikipedia.org/wiki/I-card

21. Lisa Carey: "Information Card Foundation and How it Can Protect You on Line," Discovery Articles, July 14, 2008. Online at: http://www.discoveryarticles.com/articles/140318/1/Information-Card-Foundation-and-How-it-Can-Protect-You-on-Line/Page1.html

22. For a more exhaustive treatment of this subject, see John Henry Clippinger: "A Crowd of One" (New York: Public Affairs, 2007), pp. 181-188, 194.

23. Clark Hoyt: "When Bad News Follows You," *New York Times*, Aug. 27, 2007. Online at: http://www.nytimes.com/2007/08/26/opinion/26pubed.html

Also see J.D. Lasica's response here: http://www.socialmedia.biz/2007/08/when-bad-news-f.html

24. Susan Wu: "Virtual Goods: the next big business model," TechCrunch, June 20, 2007, at: http://www.techcrunch.com/2007/06/20/virtual-goods-the-next-big-business-model/

25. Second Life, "LindeX Market Data," at http://secondlife.com/whatis/economy-market.php

26. 23andMe website at https://www.23andme.com/

27. "Kiva.org exceeds $25 million in loans from internet community—$25 at a time," Kiva.org, April 2, 2008. Online at: http://www.kiva.org/about/release_20080402

28. "The long nimbus," *The Economist*, Oct. 23, 2008. Online at: http://www.economist.com/specialreports/displaystory.cfm?story_id=12411864

29. "Threadless Chicago" retail store page on Threadless.com website at http://www.threadless.com/retail

30. Andrew Leonard: "The world in the iPod," Salon, June 3, 2005. Online at: http://dir.salon.com/story/tech/feature/2005/06/03/portalplayer/index.html

31. J.D. Lasica: "Day 2 of Web 2.0 Summit: A look at GoodGuide," socialmedia.biz, Nov. 7, 2008, online at: http://www.socialmedia.biz/2008/11/day-2-of-web-20.html

32. "We See You. Want a List of Nearby Stores?," *Inc.* Magazine, October 2008, p. 55.

33. THINKstrategies, Inc.: "Trust.Salesforce.Com Sets Standard for Service Provider Transparency & Accountability," 2007. PDF online at: http://www.salesforce.com/assets/pdf/datasheets/ThinkStrategies_Salesforce_Profile.pdf

See trust.salesforce.com for additional information.

34. Brian Grow, Keith Epstein and Chi-Chu Tschang: "The New E-spionage Threat," April 10, 2008. Online at: http://www.businessweek.com/magazine/content/08_16/b4080032218430.htm

35. Robert McMillan, Paul Venezia, "San Francisco's mayor gets back keys to the network," IT World, July 23, 2008. Online at: http://www.itworld.com/legal/53754/san-franciscos-mayor-gets-back-keys-network

36. Jefferson Graham, "E-mail carriers deliver gifts of nifty features to lure, keep users," April 15, 2008, USA Today. The Microsoft figure includes Hotmail and its other webmail services. Article online at: http://www.usatoday.com/tech/products/2008-04-15-google-gmail-webmail_N.htm

37. Electronic Privacy Information Center: "Total 'Terrorism' Information Awareness," 2003. Online at: http://epic.org/privacy/profiling/tia/

38. J.D. Lasica, phone interview with Dennis Yu of socialmedia.com, Oct. 1, 2007.

39. Serkan Toto, "Japan's Mixi: A Social Network As A Purely Local Phenomenon," TechCrunch, July 20, 2008. Online at: http://www.techcrunch.com/2008/07/20/japans-mixi-a-social-network-as-a-purely-local-phenomenon/

40. Larry Dignan: "Cloud computing meets capitalism: We all become a business of one," ZDNet, June 10, 2008. Online at: http://blogs.zdnet.com/BTL/?p=9045

41. Federal Trade Commission: Consumer Fraid and Identity Theft Complaint Data, January - December 2007. Online at: http://www.ftc.gov/opa/2008/02/fraud.pdf

APPENDIX

White House Summit on Security and Liberty

A proposal from the Seventeenth Annual
Aspen Institute Roundtable on Information Technology

The roundtable participants propose the convening of a White House Summit on Security and Liberty.

Objective: To protect personal privacy while enhancing security.

Statement: People, companies and the government want and need a society with both personal privacy and security. We believe it is now possible to achieve both goals without the need to abandon one for the other. As citizens, we want to ensure that all Americans enjoy the everyday benefits of a free society with trust, accountability, confidence and integrity as fundamental precepts.

Deliverables: The goal of the Summit will be not to issue a report or whitepaper but to produce an open source standard, supported by a policy and legal framework, for authentication and credentialing of individuals without exposing personal identifying information. Such an authentication system is needed to address issues around:

- digital identity/real ID,
- identity theft,
- cyber security and cryptography, and
- website tracking and targeted advertising.

At the same time, the framework will support the availability to law enforcement of relevant personal or identifying information upon presentation of a valid warrant.

We recommend that a multistakeholder process be formalized under the coordination of a senior White House official.

Participants: Participants to be drawn from:

    Industry

    Academia

    Health care

    Technology and telecommunications companies

    Privacy and consumer groups

    Intelligence agencies

    Department of Defense

    Department of Homeland Security

    Media organizations

    Financial services companies

    Nongovernmental organizations

    Web 2.0 companies, especially online networks

    Congressional representatives and staff

    Members of state legislatures

    Standards bodies

The Seventeenth Annual Aspen Institute Roundtable on Information Technology

Identity in the Age of Cloud Computing: Implications for Social Interaction, Governance and Money

Aspen, Colorado • July 29–August 1, 2008

Roundtable Participants

Arturo Artom
President
Netsystem
 and
President and Chief
 Executive Officer
Your Truman Show

Rod Beckstrom
Director
The National Cyber
 Security Center
United States Department
 of Homeland Security

Mark Bregman
Chief Technology Officer
Symantec

John Seely Brown
Independent Co-Chair
Deloitte Center for Edge
 Innovation
Director Emeritus
Xerox Palo Alto Research Center
 (PARC)

Daniel Burton
Senior Vice President
 of Global Public Policy
Salesforce.com

John Clippinger
Senior Fellow
The Berkman Center for
 Internet & Society

Note: Titles and affiliations are as of the date of the conference.

85

William (Bill) T. Coleman III
Founder, Chairman and
  Chief Executive Officer
Cassatt Corporation

Jeffrey Dachis
CEO in Residence
Austin Ventures

Michael DeNoma
Group Executive Director,
  Consumer Banking
Standard Chartered PLC

Esther Dyson
Chairman
EDventure Holdings

Charles M. Firestone
Executive Director
Communications and
  Society Program
The Aspen Institute

Arjun Gupta
Founder & Managing Partner
TeleSoft Partners

Aedhmar Hynes
Chief Executive Officer
Text100 Public Relations

Bradford Johnson
Principal
McKinsey & Company, Inc.

David Kirkpatrick
Senior Editor
Internet and Technology
Fortune Magazine

J.D. Lasica *(rapporteur)*
Chief Executive
socialmedia.biz

Anna Lysyanskaya
Associate Professor of
  Computer Science
Brown University

Max Mancini
Senior Director of Mobile,
  Platform and Disruptive
  Innovation
eBay Inc.

James Manyika
Director
McKinsey & Company, Inc.

Harriet P. Pearson
Vice President,
  Regulatory Policy and
  Chief Privacy Officer
IBM

Paul M. Romer
Professor
Graduate School of Business
Stanford University

Marc Rotenberg
Executive Director
Electronic Privacy Information
  Center

The Honorable Lucio Stanca
Vice-Chairman
Aspen Institute Italia
  and
Member of the Italian Parliment

Note: Titles and affiliations are as of the date of the conference.

Kim Taipale
Founder and Executive Director
The Center for Advanced Studies
  in Science and Technology

Hal Varian
Chief Economist
Google

Christine Varney
Partner
Hogan and Hartson LLP

Padmasree Warrior
Chief Technology Officer
Cisco Systems

Ann Winblad
Co-Founder and Managing
  Director
Hummer Winblad Venture
  Partners

Observer:

Angelo Maria Petroni
Secretary General
Aspen Institute Italia

Staff:

Kiahna Williams
Project Manager
Communications and
  Society Program
The Aspen Institute

Note: Titles and affiliations are as of the date of the conference.

About the Author

One of the earliest social media strategists, **J.D. Lasica** works with Fortune 500 companies as well as mid-size companies, startups and nonprofits. He is widely considered one of the world's leading authorities on social media and the revolution in user-created media.

He is chief executive of socialmedia.biz, a firm offering social media solutions to businesses and organizations that want to use social media, video and online communities to build customer relationships, promote brands and deliver value. He is also founder of Socialbrite.org, a social enterprise offering a learning center and strategic solutions to nonprofits and social causes.

His 2005 book "Darknet" (Wiley & Sons), which coined the term "personal media revolution," explores the emerging media landscape. In March 2005 he cofounded Ourmedia.org, the first grassroots media hosting and sharing site. In 2008 he was the chief architect of MediaMobz.com, a marketplace for getting videos produced.

His previous reports for the Aspen Institute include "The Mobile Generation: Global Transformations at the Cellular Level" and "Civic Engagement on the Move: How Mobile Media Can Serve the Public Good."

J.D. was also a member of senior management in three tech startups as well as a senior writer for Engadget, where he interviewed tech CEOs about new technologies. In a previous life, he spent 11 years at *The Sacramento Bee* as an editor and columnist. J.D. was among the charter members of the Online News Association.

His blog socialmedia.biz was named the No. 1 social media site in a list of the Top 100 social media websites, and he has conducted more than 200 video interviews with movers and shakers in the tech and media industries. He lives in the San Francisco area and is a frequent speaker and panelist at technology and new media conferences. Remarkably, he welcomes email at *jdlasica@gmail.com*.

Previous Publications
from the Aspen Institute
Roundtable on Information Technology

The Rise of Collective Intelligence: Decentralized Co-creation of Value (2007)

David Bollier, rapporteur

The 2007 Roundtable convened 27 leaders to analyze the current and future social and economic impacts the co-creation of knowledge across networks made possible with new communications and information technologies. While collaborative engagement encourages increased productivity and creativity, it can also lead to mass chaos from the co-creation process. The roundtable participants discussed what separates successes from failures in the new collaborative era by reviewing business and organizational models and the implications of new models. 64 pages, ISBN Paper 0-89843-481-5, $12.00 per copy.

The Mobile Generation: Global Transformations at the Cellular Level (2006)

J.D. Lasica, rapporteur

The 2006 Roundtable examined the profound changes ahead as a result of the convergence of wireless technologies and the Internet. The Roundtable addressed the technological and behavioral changes already taking place in the United States and other parts of the world as a result of widespread and innovative uses of wireless devices; the trends in these behaviors, especially with the younger generation; and what this could mean for life values in the coming decade. The Roundtable tackled new economic and business models for communications entities, social and political ramifications, and the implications for leaders in all parts of the world. 66 pages, ISBN Paper 0-89843-466-1, $12.00 per copy.

When Push Comes to Pull: The New Economy and Culture of Networking Technology (2005)

David Bollier, rapporteur

The author considers how communications, economics, business, cultural, and social institutions are changing from mass production to an individualized "pull" model. When Push Comes to Pull describes the coexistence of both push (top down or hierarchical) and pull (bottom up or networked) models—how they interact, evolve, and overlay each other in the networked information economy. The report explores the application of "pull" to the worlds of business and economics; the content and intellectual property industries; the emergence of an economy of the commons; and personal and social dynamics, including leadership in a pull world. It also touches on the application of the pull model to learning systems; the military, in the form of network-centric warfare; and the provision of government services. 78 pages, ISBN Paper 0-89843-443-2, $12.00 per copy.

Information Technology and the New Global Economy: Tensions, Opportunities, and the Role of Public Policy (2004)

David Bollier, rapporteur

This report provides context and insight into the unfolding of new economic realities arising from the information revolution—how the world's players will live, learn, innovate, offer, consume, thrive, and die in the new global economic landscape. *Information Technology and the New Global Economy* draws a portrait of a changing global economy by describing new business models for the networked environment, exploring topics of innovation and specialization. Among the more creative concepts propounded at the Roundtable was an analysis of the world's economy in terms of video game theory that suggests that if developing countries are not incorporated into the world economic community in some acceptable way—if they cannot make economic progress—they could become disrupters to the entire economic or communications system. The report also explores issues of outsourcing and insourcing in the context of digital technologies moving work to the worker instead of vice versa. Participants concentrated on developments in India and China, taking note of some of the vulnerabilities in each of those countries as well as the likely impact of their rapid development on the broader global economy. 57 pages, ISBN Paper: 0-89843-427-0, $12.00 per copy.

People / Networks / Power: Communications Technologies and the New International Politics (2003)

David Bollier, rapporteur

This report explores the sweeping implications of information technology for national sovereignty, formal and informal diplomacy, and international politics. Bollier describes the special challenges and new rules facing governments and nongovernmental organizations in projecting their messages globally. The author further explores the relationships between the soft power of persuasion and the more traditional hard power of the military and discusses how governments will have to pay close attention to newly burgeoning social communities in order to prosper. 68 pages, ISBN Paper: 0-89843-396-7, $12.00 per copy.

The Rise of Netpolitik: How the Internet Is Changing International Politics and Diplomacy (2002)

David Bollier, rapporteur

How are the Internet and other digital technologies changing the conduct of world affairs? What do these changes mean for our understanding of power in international relations and how political interests are and will be pursued? *The Rise of Netpolitik* explores the sweeping implications of information technology for national sovereignty, formal and informal international diplomacy, politics, commerce, and cultural identity. The report begins with a look at how the velocity of information and the diversification of information sources are complicating international diplomacy. It further addresses geopolitical and military implications, as well as how the Internet is affecting cross-cultural and political relationships. It also emphasizes the role of storytelling in a world in which the Internet and other technologies bring our competing stories into closer proximity with each other and stories will be interpreted in different ways by different cultures. 69 pages, ISBN Paper: 0-89843-368-1, $12.00 per copy.

The Internet Time Lag: Anticipating the Long-Term Consequences of the Information Revolution (2001)

Evan Schwartz, rapporteur

Some of the unintended consequences of the Internet and the freedoms it symbolizes are now rushing to the fore. We now know that the network of terrorists who attacked the World Trade Center and the Pentagon made full use of communication technologies, including email, Travelocity.com, automatic teller machines (ATMs), data encryption, international money transfers, cell phones, credit cards, and the like. Is the Internet an epochal invention, a major driver of the economy for many years to come, or just a passing fad? Will the new phenomena of recent years—such as the contraction of hierarchies, instant communication, and lightning-fast times to market—last beyond the funding bubble? What is the next new economy? What are the broader social consequences of the answers to those earlier questions? This report takes a wide-ranging look at the economic, business, social, and political consequences of the Internet, as well as its ramifications for the process of globalization. 58 pages, ISBN Paper: 0-89843-331-2, $12.00 per copy.

Uncharted Territory: New Frontiers of Digital Innovation (2001)
  David Bollier, rapporteur

This report looks critically at key insights on the new economy and its implications in light of the digital revolution. The report begins with an examination of the interplay between the current economy and the capital economy and then probes the emerging world of mobile commerce and its potential for driving the next great boom in the economy. It further explores new business models resulting from the combination of mobile communications and the new economy. 68 pages, ISBN Paper: 0-89843-307-X, 12.00 per copy.

Ecologies of Innovation: The Role of Information and Communications Technologies (2000)
  David Bollier, rapporteur

This report explores the nature of innovation and the role of the information and communications sectors in fostering ecologies of innovation. In this context, the report examines the ways in which the creation of new ecologies is affecting significant societal institutions and policies, including foreign policies, industry and business structures, and power relationships. 44 pages, ISBN Paper: 0-89843-288-X, $12.00 per copy.

The Global Wave of Entrepreneurialism: Harnessing the Synergies of Personal Initiative, Digital Technologies, and Global Advance (1999)

David Bollier, rapporteur

This report examines problems arising from the growth of entrepreneurialism and digital technologies. 41 pages, ISBN Paper: 0-89843-264-2, $12.00 per copy.

The Global Advance of Electronic Commerce: Reinventing Markets, Management, and National Sovereignty (1998)

David Bollier, rapporteur

This report addresses issues of electronic commerce in the context of global marketplace impact and the transformation of national sovereignty. 64 pages, ISBN Paper: 0-89843-236-7, $12.00 per copy.

Reports can be ordered online at *www.aspeninstitute.org* or by sending an email request to *publications@aspeninstitute.org*.

About the
Communications and Society Program

www.aspeninstitute.org/c&s

The Communications and Society Program is an active venue for global leaders and experts from a variety of disciplines and backgrounds to exchange and gain new knowledge and insights on the societal impact of advances in digital technology and network communications. The Program also creates a multi-disciplinary space in the communications policy-making world where veteran and emerging decision-makers can explore new concepts, find personal growth and insight, and develop new networks for the betterment of the policy-making process and society.

The Program's projects fall into one or more of three categories: communications and media policy, digital technologies and democratic values, and network technology and social change. Ongoing activities of the Communications and Society Program include annual roundtables on journalism and society (e.g., journalism and national security), communications policy in a converged world (e.g., the future of video regulation), the impact of advances in information technology (e.g., "when push comes to pull"), advances in the mailing medium, and diversity and the media. The Program also convenes the Aspen Institute Forum on Communications and Society, in which chief executive-level leaders of business, government and the non-profit sector examine issues relating to the changing media and technology environment.

Most conferences utilize the signature Aspen Institute seminar format: approximately 25 leaders from a variety of disciplines and perspectives engaged in roundtable dialogue, moderated with the objective of driving the agenda to specific conclusions and recommendations.

Conference reports and other materials are distributed to key policy-makers and opinion leaders within the United States and around the world. They are also available to the public at large through the World Wide Web, *www.aspeninstitute.org/c&s.*

The Program's Executive Director is Charles M. Firestone, who has served in that capacity since 1989, and has also served as Executive Vice

President of the Aspen Institute for three years. He is a communications attorney and law professor, formerly director of the UCLA Communications Law Program, first president of the Los Angeles Board of Telecommunications Commissioners, and an appellate attorney for the U.S. Federal Communications Commission.